Reporting:

The Tulsa Riot, 1921
The Armistice, 1918

The Archive of American Journalism

Theodore Roosevelt
Wilderness, Vol. 1

Lincoln Steffens
The System

Mark Twain
In Nevada

Richard Harding Davis
The Great War Reporter

Nellie Bly
Undercover: Reporting for the New York World

The Archive of American Journalism

Lincoln Steffens
Damon Runyon
Henry Stanley
Theodore Roosevelt
Richard Harding Davis
Ida Tarbell
Ray Stannard Baker
Nellie Bly
H.L. Mencken
Ambrose Bierce
Stephen Crane
Jack London
Mark Twain
Ernest Hemingway

www.historicjournalism.com

Damon Runyon

Articles/1915

The Archive of American Journalism
St. Paul, MN
2018

Note on Sources

All articles are complete and unabridged, with headlines, subheads and formatting that match those of the original publication. Note that minor edits have been made to correct obsolete spelling and punctuation. Students and researchers: these are "public domain" texts that can be freely copied, reproduced and distributed without permission or cost. Please credit The Archive of American Journalism as your source.

The Archive LLC
9269 Troon Court
Woodbury, MN 55125.

Article selection
Copyright ©2018 by Tom Streissguth

Cover Image: Casey Stengel, Brooklyn Dodgers, c. 1915; Library of Congress, Bain Collection
Page 2: Damon Runyon; Library of Congress
Page 10: Ernie Short (l.) and Grover Cleveand Alexander at the 1915 World Series; Library of Congress

ISBN: 978-0-9907137-8-4
Printed in the United States of America

Acknowledgments

For their encouragement and suggestions, sincere thanks to Mark Lerner, Gordon Hagert, Pier Gustafson, Phil Gapp, Jonathan Peacock, John Hatch, Marian Streissguth and our original founding supporters: *William F. Zeman, Phil Gapp, Walter Crowley, Adele Streissguth, Richard Prosser, Abhilash Sarhadi, James McGrath Morris*

Contents

Advance News of the Big Mill
El Paso Herald/January 20, 1915
11

Two New York Clubs Sized Up
Grand Forks Daily Herald/February 26, 1915
13

Damon Runyon's First "FIGG" On New York Giants
Grand Forks Daily Herald/March 15, 1915
14

Hard to Imagine Willard Fighting Negro Champion
Grand Forks Daily Herald/April 1, 1915
17

Heavyweight Battle Should Not Be Close
Washington Herald/April 3, 1915
20

Willard Wins Title In 26th From Johnson
Manitowoc Pilot/April 8, 1915
22

Willard May Be Harmed By Jones
Grand Forks Daily Herald/April 9, 1915
27

Caldwell May Have Good Year;
Yank Pitcher Looks Well Now
Washington Herald/May 1, 1915
29

Nationals Win Second of Series from Yanks
Washington Herald/July 2, 1915
32

McFarland and Gibbons Box Ten Fast Rounds;
Draw is Final Verdict
Washington Herald/September 12, 1915
34

Stage Premature Scene
Washington Herald/October 5, 1915.
40

Mayer Looming Up Big
Richmond Times-Dispatch/October 6, 1915
46

Bleacher Fans Await Charge on the Gates
Washington Herald/October 8, 1915
49

Breaks Of Luck Are Big Factor
Washington Herald/October 9, 1915
51

Alexander The Hope Of Phils
Washington Herald/October 11, 1915
56

Scott's Sacrifice Is A Big Factor
Washington Herald/October 12, 1915
60

Lewis Comes Through Again in the Pinch
Washington Herald/October 13, 1915
64

Native Sons of the Golden West Make Clouts, Giving Sox Series
Washington Herald/October 14, 1915
71

Coffey Beaten By Frank Moran
Washington Herald/October 20, 1915
78

Johnny Dundee The Winner Of Battle
Washington Herald/October 27, 1915
80

Gotham Gets Info On One J. Stecher
Omaha Daily Bee/December 12, 1915
81

Foreword

Damon Runyon has rightly gone down as the best sportswriter in American journalism. His columns and feature articles on baseball, football and boxing--the "fistic arts"--offer the reader not only fine and detailed description, but also a talent for surprising and colorful vocabulary. To read Runyon's accounts of sporting contests more than a century old is to return to the ring, or the ballpark, and encounter up close the great athletic talents of his time, including Jack Johnson, Jess Willard, Grover Cleveland Alexander ("the Great"), Tris Speaker, and Babe Ruth.

By 1915, Runyon was writing for the Hearst organization, the country's biggest and most influential newspaper syndicate. His work appeared in papers across the country, always featured above the fold on the first sports page, and often on the first page of the newspaper--a place of honor rarely given over to sports of any kind.

This book represents the first volume in a comprehensive collection of Runyon's journalism, which spans four decades, thousands of stories and a great variety of sporting, cultural and political subjects. All articles are reproduced as they first appeared in the cited papers, with only minor edits to correct misspellings, transposed lines and other errors that appeared in the originals.

SHORE & ALEXANDER

El Paso Herald
January 20, 1915

Advance News of the Big Mill

The rumor that a plot is on foot to dope Mr. John Johnson's tea was emphatically denied today by everybody connected with the affair, as it developed that Mr. Johnson does not drink tea. Another rumor that the fight is to be a fake was disproved in no time by your co-respondent, no less a person than Mr. Johnson himself stamping the story as a gross fabrication, wholly unjustified by the facts in the case. Mr. Johnson indignantly declared that he could not possibly lend himself to a cook-up unless the terms of his contract are made more advantageous.

The champion looks well, and says he is confident as to the outcome of the battle. He confided exclusively to your co-respondent that he anticipates knocking Mr. Willard sub-conscious with a right hand uppercut to the maxilla at half past 4 o'clock in round 12, but he requests that the public regard this information as strictly confidential until the day after the fight, as it might get back to Mexico and affect the attendance. Mr. Johnson says that up to the knockout it may be a pretty good contest, but he does not want his friends to be too sanguine on that point.

The big negro man did a lot of road work this morning, covering 40 kilometers in his new 90 horsepower automobile. He was panting a little at the finish, showing that he will need quite a lot of training, as "Beany" Walker, the Los Angeles sporting writer, who accompanied him on the jump, was scarcely breathing when they pulled up, and Mr. Walker is not in very good condition, at that.

Mr. Tad Dorgan, of the New York Journal, was an early caller at the Mr. Johnson camp today, and was greatly disappointed to find nobody home but the champion's big bull fiddle, and that was all unstrung.

Has Many Callers

    Other prominent callers at the camp today were Don Senor Ildefonso Iturbide Gomez, who formerly occupied a position in Gen. Carranza's army as a brigadier, and who dropped by to deliver the matutinal lacteal fluid; Edward Smith, of the Chicago (Illinois) American; Joe Norton, of Newark, and Don Senor Hype Igoe, of the New York Sun, who called with three little ones and found a full house present, with trainer Tom Flanagan presiding. It was a good game.

    Mr. Johnson has so far done no bag punching, but Kid Cotton is expected in a few days. The champion expresses himself as delighted with Mexico, and has taken naturally to tortillas, pesos, frijoles, pulque, tequila and all the other national pastimes of the republic. His heart is still in the United States, however, and he loves to listen to news from that country. He requested your co-respondent today to give his regards to Cook County, and to ask Mr. Samuel McVey to be sure and wear galoshes in wet weather, keep his throat muffled and avoid drafts, so as to preserve his health.

    Hal Stevens, the celebrated concessionaire at the race track where the fight is to be held, today received a new 1915 model Ever-Ready ham slicer from his father, H. M. Stevens, of Polo Grounds fame, and will meet all comers on the day of the contest at two bits (American money) per sandwich. All Texans who visit Mr. John's camp are being searched at the border.

Grand Forks Daily Herald
February 26, 1915

Two New York Clubs Sized Up

Damon Runyon Tells What Yanks and Giants Are Up Against

If Wild Bill Donovan had some of John J. McGraw's pounding powers, and John J. McGraw had a little of Wild Bill Donovan's pitching efficiency, we would have two all-fired swell b.b. clubs in this city in 1915.

For some years now McGraw's chief annoyance has been his hurling department, and this year—from this distance—it looks to be even more annoying than ever. For no protracted period during any of his various pennant drives has the Giant leader had three pitchers going at top speed at the same time. Sometimes he had two, but generally only Mathewson.

In one campaign Mathewson, Marquard and Demaree were delivering regularly for him; but Demaree has faded, Marquard may not report, and last year even the Old Marster was showing symptoms of a reduced temperature in the way of efficiency. McGraw has caulked up that horrible hole at third with Lobert, and has youngsters enough to fill in at other spots in case his veterans keep up the back pedaling pace some of them started last season, but he must find more pitchers.

Mathewson, Tesreau, Fromme and Marquard, if he reports, must be the groundwork of a new staff that will have to be framed from such as Ritter, Schauer, Schupp, Huenke, Cook and Stroud. The first three named should at least be ready this year, and the last two have had enough experience to break right in.

As for Wild Bill Donovan, he must inject some hitting into that infield. He might be able to carry Peckinpaugh and Maisel on their wonderful defensive work and speed, but he cannot carry any such light-hitting combination as Mullen, Bonne, Peck and Maisel and hope to get anywhere. Cook and Cree will hit enough, and so will Nunamaker, or Sweeney, but they would not be sufficient to carry along such a feeble infield as the Yanks had last season.

Given a little pitching, the Giants look good enough to win the National League pennant. Given two fair hitting infielders and another slugging outfielder, the Yanks can finish in the first division.

Grand Forks Daily Herald
March 15, 1915

Damon Runyon's First "FIGG" On New York Giants

Chances of Team for 1915 Pennant Center in Four Infielders

Let us now commence to do a little "figg" on the chances of the New York Giants in the pennant race of 1915; but let us first get right out of the dining room of the Arlington hotel, where, at this particular supper-time writing, a large posse of John J. McGraw's fresh-laid recruits are gnawing their devious ways through the menu card.

Let us leave the dining chamber, because a casual glance convinces us that there is nothing here present that might furnish us a start in our figuring on the chances of the New York Giants in the pennant race of 1915. These recruits are all very interesting, and promising, and healthy, and eat heartily, but New York pennants are not won in the gastronomical department.

Let us go out into the lobby, far from the feeding throng, and there sit down and carefully contemplate the chances of the New York Giants in the pennant race of 1915 at close range.

Let us observe Chance Merkle, as he sits poring over his interminable checker game with OP Chris Mathewson: and let us take a good, long look at Chance Doyle, and Chance Fletcher, and Chance Lobert, as they lounge in picturesque attitudes about the lobby.

First Survey of Giants' Infielders

We might have a look at Chris Mathewson, too, as he senilely shoves his checkers from port to port, and we might cast a fleeting slant at Richard W. Marquard, now mentally engrossed in the task of raising a crop of whiskers, for they come under the general head of Giant chances in the pennant pursuit of 1915; but mainly our visual survey must be centered in the four infielders of the big town club.

Dear reader, it comes as a great shock to us, as it must come as a terrible shock to you, to discover, when we commence figuring pennant chances, that all this mass of youthful brawn and bone and muscle that we have been talking about for the past few weeks can have no part in our calculations. In fact that discovery always comes as a terrible shock to us. It is not so great a shock this year as it was two years ago, because we have become somewhat calloused by constant impact of such shocks, but it is none the less a shock.

A cloud of athletic youth, a whirl of work and then a few faint flashes of promise that must be filed for future reference, and then the dust clears and the old soldiers are seen mounting guard over the various posts.

Such is the story of spring training. Such it has always been, and now that the Ides of March have come we find ourself at the task of figuring pennant chances, not on hazy possibilities, but on partly known quantities.

Has Doyle or Merkle Retrograded?

To what extent will John Honus Lobert make for the general uplift of the Giants' inner line this season? To what extent has Doyle, or Merkle, retrograded, if at all? Find the answer to these questions, and you can skip right along with the figuring to a definite conclusion without any further assistance from us.

John J. McGraw's outfield is sufficient. It may not be amazingly brilliant, but it is sufficient, no matter what shift he works. His catching will do. His pitching, as it figures out right now, with "Poll" Perritt added to the staff, should be enough. Arthur Fletcher is at the height of his big league career.

Let Doyle return to his old hitting form; let Merkle be even as good as he was last season, and let Honus Lobert soothe that aching void at third base—and the Giants will be showing the way many a time during 1915, whether or not they finally win out.

Lobert is no youngster, but so far has shown no traces of slowing up. Always a mighty runner, he is today stepping along the base paths with more speed than any man in camp, and he is hardly fully conditioned as yet. He seems to range as far and as wide around third as ever.

Lobert Best at Third Base

Last season Milton Stock and Eddie Grant together could not space out that empty stretch left by the departure of Charley Herzog and Arthur Shafer, but Lobert at his best was better than any of the four and probably has lost little of his ability.

With Mathewson and McGraw, Merkle and Doyle are now among the pioneers of the Marlin camp. They are the sole survivors of 1908, the year that James Hopper wrote of Larry Doyle, "It's great to be young and a Giant."

Since then Doyle has taken on a few gray hairs and a little weight; McGraw's hair is almost white and his corporosity increasing. But Mathewson and Merkle seem little changed, according to those who remember them as they were the first year here.

Doyle has fallen far from his mauling mark of his earlier days, but his fielding has diminished little, if any. The automobile accident of a year or so ago left his shoulder lame, and all last season he was handicapped in his hitting by the injury, but this spring he reported sound and well, and until today showed no trace of lameness. This afternoon he was favoring his arm in his throwing, and he is not going to Dallas with the regulars tonight, but the trouble is due more to overexertion than anything else. It is believed that the soreness will work out in a few days and the arm be as well as ever.

Grand Forks Daily Herald
April 1, 1915

Hard To Imagine Willard Fighting Negro Champion

So Declares Damon Runyon—Law of Ring Against Johnson

Those who retain a memory of Jess Willard in the ring find it mighty hard to conjure up a picture of the stilt-legged, scared-eyed Kansan making a real fight against the bulbous black champion at Havana Monday.

He may do it, of course. Willard may go tearing into Johnson at the tap of the gong with all the fury of an exasperated giraffe, which is a species of exasperation we have never observed, but which is the only simile we can think of in connection with Willard, exasperated or otherwise; but if he does—if Willard does this thing—he will be going contrary to all the laws of that beneficent nature which intended him to be just a large, strong, healthy specimen of humanity with no traits of violence.

He may do it, all right, and we hope he does, for it would be an imposing spectacle, but it is hard to brush away the recollection of Jess's singularly mild and inoffensive countenance, with his mouth gaping wide in a foolish grin and his gloved hands fumbled futilely before him as if to ward off an attack without any resentment—which is our chief recollection of the jayhawker in the role of a fighting man.

It is hard to brush away that recollection, and to replace it with a mental photo of this gangling, awkward string of humanity charging boldly up against that great black barrier to the hopes of our well-known white race known as John Arthur Johnson.

Here you have a hastily manufactured, practically inexperienced fellow lashing out with wild wallops at one of the greatest exponents of defensive fighting that the ring has ever known; a fighter who has behind him years and years of fistic warfare; a finished phase of the Marquis of Queensberry code, turned and polished in the mill of his craft, and yet we are expected to believe that the novice has a chance.

Law of Ring Against Johnson

We are not only expected to believe it, but, speaking for ourself, we do believe it—to a certain extent. We believe it because we believe that the law of the prize ring is against the champion. It is history that a fighting man, no matter how good he may be in the days of his youth, can't travel far beyond thirty-five before he bows down beneath the burden of life—especially that manner of life which champions generally lead.

Many people believe that if Willard beats Johnson at Havana Monday it will not be because Willard is a great fighting man, but because he is lucky enough to get the opportunity of meeting Johnson—with some credit, or discredit, in whatever light you may view those things, to his handlers for working up the opportunity. In short, they believe that if Jess Willard beats Johnson it will not be because he is Jess Willard, but because Johnson has finished out the span allotted to champions.

This is being a bit forehanded with the knock that will inevitably follow a Willard victory, to be sure, but it nevertheless reflects some of the public opinion on the coming match. Fight followers who have seen Willard in the ring cannot, by any stretch of the imagination, think of him as a great fighter, but they concede him a chance Monday. They would concede any one of half a dozen strong young fellows now classed as white hopes a chance, because the law of the old game is against Johnson.

Has Ten Years on Champion

Willard is ten years younger than the champion, and yet Willard is no youngster, as youngsters go in the prize ring. He is crowding 28. There is a wide difference in the fighting game between 30 and 37, but it would be all the wider in the present case had Willard begun his fighting earlier. He started at an age when many a fighter has finished his career in the ring, and it may be that he began too late.

His size and his presumed strength have often been cited in his favor. As a matter of fact, some good judges of fighting men believe that he is too big for fighting purposes. His strength can always come in handy, but his strength is really an unknown quantity. Willard has bowled over a few of the genus "sucker" in the ring, and it is believed that he can punch, but no one knows whether he can punch a good man because he never punched at a good man. He never had the opportunity.

Johnson Has Great Left Hand

It is pointed out that his height will handcuff Johnson's murderous right uppercut, the pointers evidently over-looking the fact that Johnson has a pretty good left hand. It has been said that both Johnson and Willard are strictly "waiters"; that they hang back waiting for the other fellow to come in, which, if true, would argue a tedious time at Havana next week, but as a matter of fact the big black has often stepped out after his man, shuffling along the canvas until he gets in striking range.

The chances are he will go after Willard, and the chances are that Willard will not be able to keep him from catching up. Jess has never displayed any light and airy foot faculties hereabouts. He has merely shown a painful hesitancy about slamming a man, hovering mildly out of reach of the gloves until he happens to get stung, and then suddenly waking up and rushing in with a fierce flailing of his long arms.

He has been able to hit the men he has fought in the past, but there is some doubt as to his ability to hit Johnson, and there is no doubt as to Johnson's ability to hit Jess. It all simmers down, so far as Willard's chances are concerned, to a question of Jess's ability to assimilate all of Johnson's hitting until such time as Jack is footsore and wearied of his task. In other words, it seems to simmer down to a question of condition and endurance.

And then, again, Willard may knock Johnson kicking in the early rounds; or Johnson may dispose of Willard so rapidly as to make the Munroe-Jeffries fiasco seem like a marvelous event, all of which will be additional proof of what fools us prophets be.

Washington Herald
April 3, 1915

Heavyweight Battle Should Not Be Close

Damon Runyon Claims Willard Does Not Start to Compare with Jack Johnson

It seems to be generally accepted by nearly all the Americans in Cuba as an almost foregone conclusion that Jess Willard will beat Jack Johnson. Yet, on the strength of their work-outs today, with Johnson in good condition, it should not be even close.

There is as much difference between the men as between a skilled workman and an apprentice.

As old as he is, Johnson has forgotten more of the method and manner of the Queensbury code than Willard ever will learn.

Willard may have acquired a few gymnasium tricks that make him shape up a little better to the eye than ever before and he is certainly in grand physical condition, but, in the main, he is about the same gangling, ungraceful fellow that was known to the New York ring followers a few months ago.

His improvement strikes one as largely superficial. He still boxes from an awkward straddle-legged position, with his mouth hanging open, his right hand drawn back as if about to throw a rock.

He still flares up occasionally as if in an excess of fury, charges in and roughs it with his sparring partner and then, at the height of the milling his good nature reasserts itself and the bland face cracks in smiles. He seems to have developed a good snap to his left hand punches, but he never has much of an idea of what will be at the end.

The champion slammed his sparring partners, Colin Bell, "Steamboat Bill" Scott and Dave Mills around until he was streaked with perspiration. He went eight minutes with Bell at top speed, without stopping and displaying all his cleverness.

Apparently for Gibbons' benefit, Johnson laughed and kidded throughout, asking Gibbons such questions as "How's that, for a fat man."

His torso, from the hips to the shoulders is as level as the flanks of a fatted steer, but he had his sparring partners smashing him in the stomach as an answer to a remark of a spectator about his waist line.

Johnson's doctor claims that his pulse never shows any indication that his wind is affected even after the most grueling workout, but it was noticed that when the champion talked to spectators after the drill today he seemed to be making an extra exertion to breathe through the nose, with the muscles of his stomach throbbing like a man under some stress.

"Tom" Flanagan was around today hunting some even money and claiming that should be the logical price because Johnson is an old man.

Despite the strong tip that is out on Willard little money is in sight on either man. It is hard to explain the wild rush of sentiment to Willard, save on the ground of his condition.

It is said the promoters are sure they can show the pictures in America if Willard wins, despite the laws on the subject.

The usual talk of "fake" that has preceded every big fight is heard. There are weird tales of early morning training by Johnson, followed by indolence in the public workouts to beat down the betting price, but if Johnson is doing any early morning work it does not show in his appearance.

Big crowds of men and women saw the fighters today.

Victor Munioz, the famous sporting editor of the El Mundo, says the Cubans are taking a great interest in the fight, but that the crowd would have been twice as large had it been held on Sunday. Indications are that not to exceed 3,000 Americans from the states will be here, if that many.

It is said that Harry Frazee, one of the promoters, has announced that he will hire a special train from Key West if Willard wins.

Manitowoc Pilot
April 8, 1915

Willard Wins Title In 26th From Johnson

Youth Is Too Much for Negro Pugilist

Right To Jaw Wins Battle

Black Had Better of Argument to Twentieth, But Rapidly Lost Ground Thereafter Before Cowboy's Fierce Rushes

Jess Willard, a gawky, green-looking Kansas farmer and cowpuncher, is champion of the world with all the world before him while Jack Johnson, late lord of the pugilistic realm, is just a portly, middle-aged colored man browsing on the memory of one of the greatest battles ever made by a fighter of his years.

One ferocious right hand smash to the pit of Johnson's fat black stomach that crumpled the big body of the negro in grinding pain at the opening of the twenty-sixth round followed half a minute later by a terrific right hand clip to the jaw, are the blows that made new history for the American sport on alien soil, with alien tongues drowning the sound of American voices in the weird demonstration that followed.

Johnson fell and was counted out by Referee Jack Welch in his own corner.

Johnson did not seem to be totally unconscious, recovering soon after his seconds gathered him up.

Cuban soldiers had to pile into the ring with drawn sabers to rescue both of the fighters from the crush.

Round 1—Johnson feinted and landed his left on Willard's jaw. He sent right uppercut to jaw, Willard was nervous, and Johnson was laughing. Willard got in two to body and Johnson retaliated with a jolt to Jess' body.

Round 2—Johnson blocked two swings for the head. Johnson grinned again. Willard landed left on Johnson's body. Johnson landed three on Willard's ribs in quick succession. Willard swung and Johnson ducked, coming back with a swing that hit Willard in the face. Willard swung right to the body.

Round 3—Willard made two swings but both missed. Johnson aimed his left for the body but Willard blocked neatly. Willard rushed the negro but missed another swing. They clinched. Johnson drove Willard to the ropes with five successive body blows. Johnson broke through Willard's guard, landing blows rapidly upon the white man's heart. Then he jabbed Willard's face. Johnson landed right on body and then began kidding the challenger. Johnson landed a blow to the jaw and one to the head. Johnson drove Willard to the ropes with a shower of punches as the round ended. Johnson's round.

Round 4—Johnson blocked three lefts by Willard. The negro blocked two more and then they clinched. Jack landed his right to the body. Johnson ducked Willard's swing which drove him to the ropes. Willard landed two blows to the body. Johnson landed to the stomach and tried for the jaw, but was blocked. Willard missed a swing. Jack landed one in the face. End of round. Shade for Willard.

Round 5—Willard landed to the face. Johnson's mouth is bleeding. Johnson shot his left into Willard's body and followed with his right to the face. The negro ducked Willard's right swing and landed three punches on Willard's body. Johnson landed three hard blows. Willard landed one on Johnson's body in return. Jess drove Johnson to the ropes as the round ended. Willard's round.

Round 6—Willard took the offensive but missed a swing for the head. Jack drove Willard against the ropes with punches to the head. Johnson then landed a terrific left on Willard's body, following with a punch just below the heart. Johnson drove left and right to the body, then another right to the body.

Round 7—Johnson blocked Willard's left. They clinched. Johnson landed his left to the body, sending Jess to the ropes. Willard landed his right to Johnson's jaw. Johnson then rushed Willard to the ropes after drawing a leading. Willard missed with his right but landed left on Jack's body. Johnson again drove Willard to the ropes as the round ended. Johnson's round.

Round 8—Johnson landed his left on Willard's jaw. Willard landed his right on Johnson's body. The negro came back with two body punches, both landing. Johnson cut Willard's ear and then landed again on his head. Willard's round.

Round 9—Willard rushed but Jack blocked four swings for the head. Willard finally landed his right on Jack's heart. Johnson whipped a smash to the stomach and Willard returned with a right to Jack's jaw. Johnson landed left on the body and once more drove Willard to the ropes. Round even.

Round 10—Willard forced the fighting and landed left to Jack's face. Johnson drove Willard to the ropes with body punches. Jack jabbed Jess in the face three times. Johnson drove Willard to the ropes with a volley of blows to the face. The negro landed his right on Willard's body, following with a terrific right to the jaw. He was trying for a knockout. Johnson's round.

Round 11—Johnson, forcing the fighting, landed on Willard's head. They clinched. Willard returned a right to the body. Jack again drove a right to the body. Johnson drove his left to Willard's face and ducked Willard's right. The negro landed two more body blows. Jess countered to the body. Johnson landed on Willard's stomach. Even round.

Round 12—Johnson went after Willard and landed two to the body. Willard missed a terrific right to the head. Johnson ducked easily. Coming up from the duck Johnson smashed Willard's face with rights and lefts and then landed left to the body. Willard countered with two to body. Johnson then landed four on Willard's head, driving him back against the ropes. Johnson's round.

Round 13—Johnson again started with grim eagerness, landing two to the body before Willard swung a healthy right to the stomach. Johnson shot a left to the jaw. Jack then smashed with all his might with a left to the body and repeated. Willard swung wildly and Jack blocked another swing. Johnson's round.

Round 14—Willard missed three circling swings. Jack landed left to body. They smothered up in a clinch. Willard landed left to the head after they broke and Johnson slammed his left into Willard's body. Johnson's round.

Round 15—Johnson rushed Willard to the ropes. As Jess went back he put a right to Jack's abdomen and then smashed

Jack's kidneys. He drove a left to Willard's face and sent Jess back to the ropes with a shower of lefts and rights. A smashing drive to Willard's stomach followed the rain of punches. Johnson's round.

Round 16—Johnson continued his desperate efforts to win with a knockout. He landed a right to the body and a left to the head and continually kept on top of Willard, landing whenever an opening appeared. Willard fought back strongly. Willard took two lefts to the body just as the bell rang. Johnson's round.

Round 17—After landing on the cowboy's face with a left Johnson easily avoided a wild swing and sent a right to the face. Willard came back with two rights to the body and a left to the face and clinched after Johnson got in a left. Johnson shot a terrific right to the body. Willard smashed his right to the body. Even.

Round 18—Jack easily ducked a couple of swings and put over three to the body. Johnson's round.

Round 19—Johnson was tiring, but blocked a Willard swing and countered with a left to the body. Jack's speed was decreasing. They exchanged blows, Jack getting in a left to the head and taking a right to the body. An even exchange of half a dozen blows followed. As the gong rang Willard's right caught Jack's head and Johnson shot in a right and left to the head. Even round.

Round 20—Johnson sprang from his corner and landed a left to the face. Then he missed five successive swings. Willard landed a right to the body, and then Johnson chased Jess around the ring. He landed several blows to the cowboy's head, while Willard drove his right and left to the body. Johnson's round.

Round 21—Jack drove a right and left to Willard's body, but Jess countered with a right to the head. Jack sent another right to the face. Round even.

Round 22—Willard took the lead, jabbing his left to Johnson's face. They clinched and Johnson took six punches on the stomach. Willard swung his right and missed. Willard's round.

Round 23—Willard sent a left to Johnson's body, but Jack then blocked five swings. Jack landed three lefts to the body, one of the swats glancing off Willard's shoulder. Willard drove to the face and repeated the blow. Willard's round.

Round 24—Johnson opened with a left to the body and took one in return. Jack landed another left and blocked a jab.

They went into a clinch. Willard landed a left to the face. Johnson sent a right to the body and a left to the face and took two lefts to the face. Round even.

Round 25—Willard got in his first good punch, a terrific right to the body. Willard forced the fighting and Johnson showed he was tiring. Willard landed a right to the jaw and followed with two lefts to the face, easily winning the honors for the session. Willard's round.

Round 26—Referee Welch stepped over to Johnson and motioned him to the center of the ring. Willard stood ready to meet the dimming champion. As Johnson came within reach Willard tore loose with the fury of a wildcat. He whipped in a right to the body and a left to the face. A right crashed on the colored battler's jaw. It slowed him up and he hung on. Suddenly Johnson started a left jab, but he faltered and missed. Willard was gone from the spot at which the blow was directed, and again the negro's arm dropped. Willard set himself and Johnson's arm went up in defense, but an instant too late. Willard drove through his man-killing right to the chin and Johnson staggered about the ring, his arms dangling. He tried instinctively to gather himself together. Willard again started his right for the title-holder's vulnerable spot. The glove that carried almost superhuman strength behind it reached Johnson's jaw with a thud. The colored man's eyes rolled and blinked as he dropped to the canvas, where he lay crumpled, as the referee tolled off the fatal count.

Grand Forks Daily Herald
April 9, 1915

Willard May Be Harmed By Jones

Manager Has Habit, Says Runyon, of Making Champions Unpopular

The big fight is over, and the white race is some race, boys. It was reported that there is some dissension among the syndicaters of Willard over the question of the proprietorship of Big Jess.

The men who put up the money for the fight and Jack Curley, who was the truck horse of the occasion, are said to have been laboring under the delusion that they had an interest in Willard's subsequent efforts; while Tom Jones, manager of the Kansan, is alleged to have taken the ground that the syndicate is concerned only with the pictures and has nothing whatever to do with Willard himself.

If the report is true, this little matter promises a large amount of conversation from both sides in the immediate future. If the promoters did not know just where they stood in the premises, it was their own fault, for they cannot say they did not know T. Jones, whose generosity is proverbial in the sporting world. Thomas will give you two nickels for a quarter any time.

Willard makes Jones's third champion, Papke and Wolgast being the others. When a man comes up with that many money-getters the sporting fraternity is apt to argue that he is lucky, but we are inclined to the belief that in Jones's case it represents an innate genius for avoiding work.

Jones Develops Champions

Jones is unquestionably a good developer of fighters; but while he is able to make champions, he does not possess the faculty of making champions particularly popular.

Willard is a fellow whose appearance and personality should bring him great popularity during his championship career;

but it would not be at all surprising to see Jones adopt a course that will eventually have just the opposite effect.

It is said that Jones plans to have Willard work the theaters for a couple of years, and most judges of fighters believe that this will be fatal to Jess's ring life.

In the first place, the Kansan is twenty-seven years old, which is none too young for a fighter, because he is nearing that stage when the weight he picks up is likely to become plastered to the ribs. Willard is already showing a tendency to take on weight, and two years of comparative idleness would have him as big as a house. In the second place, unless he does some fighting the sporting public is practically certain to raise the cry that he beat an old man and is not a real champion.

Still Lacks Experience

Another thing, Willard does not know enough about fighting as yet to be able to afford to keep out of the ring. He is a very crude state in every way, and it is going to take a lot of drilling to smooth off the rough edges.

Jones has an inflated idea of Willard's stage value, as is indicated by the fact that he told one man who today offered him $3,500 a week that he expected to get a thousand dollars a day for Jess's services. Jones feels that the vaudeville houses are altogether too small for the business he is going to do, anyway, and is talking about Madison Square Garden.

Photographs of the knockout were sold around Havana at $3 each, and the first supply was soon exhausted. The pictures show that as Johnson lay flat on his back in Willard's corner, with Welch counting over him, the negro had his gloved hands raised over his face as if to protect his eyes from the blinding sun, and while this movement may have been involuntary, it is taken by many to indicate that Johnson was not totally unconscious.

Some believe that when he went to the floor he could have gotten up again and gone along a couple of rounds more., but that he realized it would be a useless effort and so took the count to avoid being unduly battered.

Washington Herald
May 1, 1915

Caldwell May Have Good Year

Yank Pitcher Looks Well Now

Caldwell's Temperament, Which Caused Frank Chance to Land on Him, Finally Causing Him to Jump to Feds, Doesn't Worry Wild Bill Donovan at All, and Caldwell Is Pitching High Class Ball.

There has never been any particular doubt in the minds of the followers of baseball hereabouts as to the status of Ray Caldwell, so far as pitching ability is concerned. He has long been generally recognized as one of the very best when he is "going good," as the pastimers say, but with some inflection on the when.

In point of natural pitching gifts the Human Hairpin of the Yanks rank with Mathewson, Alexander, or Johnson. He has lacked only their steadiness of purpose in the past to make him just as valuable to his club and just as famous through the land.

Last year Caldwell started out with a run of victories that he might have parlayed into a very wonderful record before the close of the season, but he was abducted by the Feds, remained idle for weeks, and his accomplishments were almost forgotten in the subsequent flurry of events. Even so, however, he bobs up in the archives with a mighty good showing. He worked in 31 games before he departed, and finished seventh, in point of effectiveness, among the hurlers of the American league.

Those who are familiar with the affairs of the Yanks say that the ex-telegrapher quit the club because he felt that he was ill-1treated by Frank Chance, whose habit it was to slap fines on Ray whenever the long fellow incurred the managerial displeasure. Frank, probably, has his side of the matter, but the result indicated that this was not exactly the way to handle Caldwell, and the Yanks temporarily lost the services of a great pitcher.

We are informed that Ray tends somewhat to the temperamental, and Chance never could abide temperament. It was his firm, old fashioned opinion that an ellum club was the greatest cure in the world for temperamental ball players, and he probably believes to this day that only the Society for the Prevention of Mayhem to Pastimers prevented him from stamping out all temperament in the large leagues.

On the other hand, Wild Bill Donovan does not mind temperament at all. Wild Bill Donovan can eat and sleep right alongside old Temperament and never get any wilder, and that is perhaps the reason that he is able to coax two-hit games out of the temperamental Ray Caldwell.

More About Temperament

When we say that Ray is temperamental we do not mean to convey that his customs in private life are such as would be disapproved by Billy Sunday. A ballplayer may have temperament without bad habits—or, at least, without any very bad habits. Tillie Shafer, for instance, had a heap of temperament, yet we have seen Tillie walk right into a church and sit down in a pew. We saw him from a crack in the front door.

Ty Cobb has temperament. So has Davy Robertson. So, in a slightly less degree, has Tris Speaker. Honus Wagner never had much temperament. All he had was a terrible wallop in his bat. Christy Mathewson is not temperamental. Richard W. Marquard, Sr., is. Rucker was always shy in that respect, and Alexander never had enough temperament to last him over night, while Sherwood Magee or Heine Zimmerman has enough to make up for the rest of the league.

Personally, Caldwell is an amiable cuss. He enjoys this business of living and he loves to live without any enemies around to harass him, and so he does not make enemies. He is glad to see Ray Caldwell doing well, but he is not uppish in the chest about it—not a bit. And he never was.

This season may prove Caldwell's best since he came into the big league. He seems perfectly satisfied with his present environment, and Wild Bill Donovan has to date made no motions at the Caldwell bankroll. Wherefore, Ray feels disposed to do a lot of pitching, and there is no denying that Ray can pitch a lot when he feels so disposed.

He was not ready Saturday, despite his great showing against the Griffmen. He was not using his fast ball at all, sticking strictly to curves, and keeping his delivery mixed up. Johnson used a fast one to considerable extent, but, oddly enough, it was his speed that the Yanks hit.

Why Not a Chance?

It is now being quite generally stated that no white man in the ring today has a chance against Jess Willard. We hold that to be an idle statement, just as we held it an idle statement that Jess had no chance against Jack Johnson, when the match was first made.

There were mightily few dissenters that the long Kansan would be a joke in front of Johnson, and there are mighty few dissenters now to the proposition that none of the other white fighters can hope to whip the Jayhawker.

Why? Is Jess going to get any younger or any better during the year or so that his handlers plan to keep him on the stage? Is it any more ridiculous to suggest that Coffey or Reich or some of these other young fellows have a chance against Willard than it was to suggest a year ago that Willard could give the black man a battle?

Willard then hardly knew one hand from the other. He was suspected by some of a saffron streak as wide as Broadway. He had fought no man of any admitted class, and, in fact, he fought no man of any admitted class up to the day he crawled through the ropes at Havana. If such an apparently hopeless hope as Jess could be worked up to the championship, it strikes us that there is a very good chance, indeed, for the others.

Curley Made the Champ

We agree with the friends of Jack Curley that he is the man responsible for making Willard champion. Regardless of any managerial acumen that may be possessed by Tom Jones, and regardless of Willard's fighting ability, he would still be the popular paragraphic jest of the hour but for Curley's efforts.

It was Curley who did all the heavy lifting in connection with the fight from start to finish. It was Curley who made the fight possible, and it may eventually be Curley who will go out and find that supposedly non-existent opponent for his handmade champ.

Washington Herald
July 2, 1915

Nationals Win Second of Series from Yanks

"Georgetown" Tommy Connolly Halts New York's Rally in Final Session and Griffmen Win, 5 to 3—Bert Gallia Shows Real Form

Among the visitors to the Polo Grounds this afternoon were the members of the varsity crew of Leland Stanford University, who finished second to Cornell up at Poughkeepsie the other day in a race that covered four miles of adjectives, and wore out more readers of the newspapers of this city than any other contest in recent years.

It is said that circumstances, and a slight absence of the old do-re-mi have left the Stanford oarsmen flat on their sun-burned backs in the effete East. The shell they shoved with such fluency down the Hudson River is still tethered to a hitching post up there in Dutchess County awaiting transportation back to dear old California.

A shell is now of no further use to them.

Yanks Left Stranded

To put it gently, the Stanford shellers are stranded. That's why they went to the pastime today. They wanted company. They found it in those Yanks. The Yanks also were stranded today. They were generally as far away from home as the Stanford lads are from Palo Alto. It must be pretty tough to be a Stanford man stranded in New York, or a Yank stranded on second base.

Of course, the Stanford lads will get home all right, and that is more than can be prophesied of the Yanks. Certainly the Yanks are permanent derelicts on the American League so far as today's pastime is concerned. It went to Ol' Clark Griffith's Washington crew by a score of 5 to 3.

Ol' Roy Hartzell earnestly endeavored to give us a Stanford finish in the ninth inning when he stepped forward and spurted a home run into the right field stand, with a gent on and no gent out, but the Yanks did not have enough vitality left to pull on past Connolly out in right field. Their stroke subsided to about twenty-one to the minute after Hartzell had lifted it up to forty-four, or thereabouts.

Uses Pinch Hitters

Coach Donovan hastily slipped two members of the Yanks' freshman eight into the home town boat in that final flurry, using Birdie Cree and Pete Daley as pinch hitters, but Connolly drifted back and forth and spongily absorbed all flies that came his way. He got Boone's hoist, which came after Hartzell's homer, and then he took care of both Daly and Cree.

This Connolly is a colleger. It is barely possible that he is even a frat-brother to some of those Stanford shell artists, but it is doubtful if he ever grew a callous in his had fondling a sweep. He acts more like a born right fielder. Ol' Clark Griffith thinks well of Connolly and discounts the fact that Con habitually employs an education in his baseball work.

Bert Gallia was the Silver Squirrel's hurler today. Bert is right handed and a member of the tall and rangy guys association. Likewise he has the hop to his fast one and can pickle that well-known cabbage—he cooked up a couple of blows for himself today. Bert has no college degree, but a man doesn't really need a degree if he has the hop to his fast one. He needs control.

Gallia opened the Washington phase of the third with a

double to left and Connolly singled. Gallia took third, and tallied when Foster forced Connolly at second. Foster stole second and took third on Howard Shanks' out, but Milan could not assist.

John Henry, Connolly, Neff, Cook, and some of the other college boys involved in the diversion yesterday could organize quite an alumni ball club. They could use Nick Altrock as the coach. Nick coaches the Navy when he is not opening and closing in one of Ol' Clark Griffith. Nick put on his act yesterday and it got over very nicely.

Washington Herald
September 12, 1915

McFarland and Gibbons Box Ten Fast Rounds; Draw is Final Verdict

Big Scrap Which Promised Much Turns Out to Be a Fizzle

Stock Yard Champ Able to Hold His Own with St. Paul Middle-weight

Along about the sixth round of the exhibition between Packey McFarland, of Chicago, and Mike Gibbons, of St. Paul, down at Brighton Beach tonight, a loud-voiced man rose from a ringside seat and let forth a roar that reverberated up and back and far out over the biggest crowd that ever saw a fistic event in America.

"Gents," said the man, hoarsely, "this is a grand picture show, but I came here to see a fight."

And from the murmur that responded to his cry it was apparent that many others present echoed those sentiments.

The McFarland-Gibbons affair may have been a fair boxing exhibition—and certainly it contained nothing that could offend the finer feelings of any of the thousands of women present—but as a fight it was not much. It was a ten-round, no-decision affair, and no decision would be about correct, but if a decision must be given, a draw is not unfair to either man.

They were both on their feet and fighting at the finish. There had been no damage inflicted on either side, and neither man had any distinct advantage at any stage of the contest.

McFarland in Comeback Role

Perhaps McFarland should have the decision for the showing that Mike Gibbons made as compared to his previous form, especially when it is considered that the Chicagoan was doing a comeback after a two years' retirement, was boxing a man reputed to be one of the greatest fighters in the world, and for the reason that Mike should have done better, but all things considered, it was an even proposition. It was in many ways a big disappointment.

Cry of "Fake" Heard

As long as it is remembered by the sporting world, there will undoubtedly be many who will claim that it was "one of those things" as matches made with a previous understanding as to the result, are called by sporting men, but there is no way of proving it.

The charge has been openly made by a recognized authority for weeks past that the men would not try tonight, and there has even been a rumor around to the effect that McFarland had made Gibbons put up a cash deposit with a mutual friend in Chicago to guarantee against a knock-out, but here again is something that cannot be substantiated.

There are always rumors of this kind going around before a big match and perhaps the only result that would have prevented criticism of the affair tonight would have been a knock-out by Gibbons. Certainly a knock-out by McFarland would have been viewed askance, and it may be that the men were trying desperately, but if so their best efforts will receive many a knock for many a day to come.

McFarland got $17,500 for this match. Gibbons received $15,000. They got the cash in advance. No phase of a championship was involved. McFarland was a supposed light-weight when he was at his best, while Gibbons rates as a middle-weight. As a sporting proposition, few critics ever saw a justification for the match, save as a money-getter, and it got the money from the public tonight.

The slashing Mike Gibbons, sometimes styled the St. Paul Phantom and the Gopher State Ghost, was unable to even outrough the Chicago man, fresh from a two-year retirement, and with a light roll of fat about his middle. It was generally figured that Packey might outbox Gibbons, because Packey was one of the cleverest men in the world, but it was thought that Mike would at least jar the pride of the stockyards with that famous man-dropping punch if he could get it over. He did get it over, but he did not get it over with any force and it failed to rock McFarland at any stage.

Terry McGovern Shakes His Head

As a little sidelight to the affair, the face of the once "Terrible Terry" McGovern, who sat right behind Gibbons' corner, was a profound study throughout the fight. The former champion and one of the greatest fighting men of his inches that ever crawled through the ropes, would look first at one and then at the other, and then he would shake his head as if he could scarcely credit what he saw.

It was not a good fight, but it was set in marvelous surroundings. It marked high tide in boxing history in point of attendance. It was held in the center of probably 50,000 people, under a star-studded sky, in sound of the ocean breakers pounding the boardwalks of Brighton, and among these 50,000 people were handsomely gowned women and whole acres of notables of the sporting, political, dramatic and social worlds. If it was as many whisper, "one of those things," it demonstrates the old adage that New York will stand for anything, for the public life of New York was strongly represented.

It would be unfair to say that everybody was dissatisfied with the bout. Many thought, and many said, that it was a good fight, but from the mouths of the wise men of the game scattered through the arena rose the sibilant whisper of suspicion, even in the first few rounds. However, at the very same moment could be heard, around the press bench, the voices of some very great sporting authorities dictating tales to their newspapers that are bound to give the readers the impression that a most thrilling struggle occurred down yonder by the waves.

The crowd exceeded all guesses. The gate receipts were above conjecture. Most sporting men thought that the Marshall brothers were insane when they paid $32,500 to the boxers besides spending at least $15,000 more to carry out the fight, but the gamble won. For a fight that had no bearing on any championship, the result was astounding.

At two minutes after 10 o'clock a roar from the crowd told of the coming of one of the principles. McFarland clambered into the ring as a wave of applause swept down over the throng. Packey was dressed in a pair of blue serge pants as he came in, and wore a jersey. His hands were bandaged. When he stripped off his pants a pair of green trunks showed. Packey weighed 152 in full ring costume and Gibbons 153. This was ringside weight.

McFarland's seconds were Johnny McFarland, his cousin: Ike Bernstein, his trainer, and Emil Thiery, his business manager. Billy Gigson, a personal friend, also attended Packey.

Gibbons came in eight minutes later and there was another burst of applause. Mike wore a pair of black pants and a gray sweater. He walked over to Packey's corner and felt of the bandages, but they exchanged not a word.

Gibbons was attended by Tom Gibbons, Billy Moore, and Marty Farrel. While the gloves were being adjusted, Thiery watched Gibbons, and Moore viewed the process in McFarland's corner.

Joe Humphreys fired more shots and announced that Dick Peters and Johnny Green would fight a ten-round go immediately after the main event.

Then he gave the weights and introduced Gibbons as the St. Paul wizard.

McFarland was presented as Chicago's fighting Irishman and received a greater reception than Mike.

At 10:12 the men stepped to the center of the ring with their handlers and received instructions from John, while a horde of photographers aimed cameras at them. After a short conversation the ring was cleared at 10:14.

The gong sounded and the men swung into fighting positions.

Gibbons was the first to lead and missed with a left. Packey was then short with a left lead and Gibbons landed a light left twice to the face. At close quarters McFarland worked two rights to body. A clinch followed, and as they broke, Gibbons sent a right to the head and they clinched.

Gibbons seemed to be a little wild when he tried a left swing and Packey reached a long left to the head.

Mike's celebrated right hand seemed to drift a little forward and beyond Packey's head, which caused a slight murmuring from the crowd.

Packey got home a nice left at the start of the next round and then got in a left hook. For a man in Mike's apparent condition, his blows seemed to lack the snap and accuracy with which the New York fight fans are familiar. Once in the second he whaled Packey on the side of the head with a right chop. Which is usually his "Sunday punch," but it seemed to drop lightly.

During the third round the crowd again began to murmur. Both got home light blows to face, but when Mike missed a right hook by a couple of feet, the murmur became very audible.

Packey hit Mike a couple of open handed punches, and there was some nice boxing at close quarters, but nothing damaging on either side.

When they dropped into a clinch in the fourth, some one yelled:

"Look at 'em talking; Oh, look at 'em."

If they were conversing, their words could not be heard.

"He's whispering right in his ear," said the same voice, meaning that Mike was doing the whispering.

"Good boy, Packey," "You've got him," came a cry from the audience as the fourth round closed, but there was a note of derision in the cry.

Crowd Becomes Peevish

The complaints of the crowd became more pronounced as the men went through the early stages of the fifth. In that round, however, Gibbons let loose a right that looked to be about the hardest punch that had been started, but it did no damage.

The old rip and dash of the St. Paul man was entirely missing. Mike has fought some corking fights around New York, and some bad ones, but up to the fifth he showed none of the class that he undoubtedly possesses when he is trying. The same might be said of McFarland. Never a hard puncher, or a knocker out, he has nevertheless displayed much more form than he displayed in the early rounds tonight.

McFarland had a shade in the fifth, however, because he did most of the leading. It was about the first round that could reasonably be given to either man.

In the sixth, McFarland hit Gibbons a little low, but apologized. There was a close exchange in McFarland's corner, but the blows that landed fell on elbows. Mike missed badly in this round, and he opened an old cut under his right eye.

In the seventh blood showed over Gibbons left eye and trickled down his nose. He had evidently been butted. Whenever they clinched thereafter Mike wiped the blood off on Packey's shoulders. Packey seemed a bit weary from the exertion, and it was Mike's round. There seemed to be more drive to his punches during this session than before. In the eighth Gibbons missed with both hands. In fact, the story would have to be a narrative of misses if an attempt were made to detail every lead.

Blows Fall Short

Blows with which Gibbons has knocked men cold, from a distance of six inches, fell without apparent weight on Packey's head.

The ninth and tenth produced more slugging than any of the other rounds. In the tenth, especially, Gibbons put some steam behind his blows, and Packey landed with more strength than usual.

The Gibbons right began dropping alongside Packey's head, and Packey fought hard in the clinches, but at the finish both men seemed fresh, and certainly neither was damaged.

When the gong sounded two loud notes at the close of the last round Packey made a move as if to hit Gbbons when Mike was walking toward his corner. Mike bristled, and there was a suggestion of further hostilities, but Packey's seconds pulled him away.

Afterward Packey walked over to Gibbons and they shook hands. Someone asked McFarland what Gibbons said to him and the Chicagoan replied:

"He said I was the best boy he ever boxed."

"Why did he say that?" demanded the interrogator.

"Because he is a gentleman," answered McFarland.

Packey remained in the ring some time after Gibbons left, posing for pictures and receiving the plaudits of the crowd.

Packey's friends were evidently firmly convinced that he had won, and Packey apparently thought so himself. He was jubilant and a little vengeful.

"Who's the big stiff now?" he asked someone in the audience, evidently meaning he had been so defined.

Washington Herald
October 5, 1915

Stage Premature Scene

Damon Runyon Fears for Success of Series

Pat Moran and Bill Carrigan Act "Hastily" at Polo Grounds Yesterday, and Result May Be "Serious"

One of the most essential and certainly one of the most solemn scenes pertaining to a well-regulated world's series was seriously damaged, if not totally ruined, by a burst of prematureness up at the Polo Grounds this afternoon. From now on we are going to feel mighty pessimistic about the success of this impending series.

It does not seem to us that you can go ahead and put on a scene as important to a world's series as this one so far in advance without taking something away from the championship contest, and certainly without this scene a world's series would be something like a New Wayburn show, sans le-er-ah-ah-limb-ah's.

Which is to say, a blank.

We refer, of course, to that scene where the managers of the opposing clubs shake hands. That is the very scene we are mumbling about, and it is a great hit and has been for years. It takes place just before the opening of the first game, and is most extemporaneous and accidental-like, with everybody else cleared away from the home plate, where it generally occurs, and with the managers holding each other's grimy right paw as if it were a dead fish, their faces cracked in alleged smiles, and their caps pushed well back from their adamant brows to give the poor lens a chance.

Premature Scene

This scene proves that despite the horrible rivalry existing between 'em, the managers are none the less sportsmen enough to extend the right hand of friendship, especially when the photographers are so insistent about it. We just naturally hate to think of a world's series without this scene, but what do you suppose occurred up at the Polo Grounds this afternoon?

Why, Pat Moran and Bill Carrigan, managers of the Phillies and the Red Sox, put on the scene several days too soon, and now it will be such old stuff for the world's series that the house manager may demand they cut it out.

Pat Moran was responsible for the prematureness. He wandered into the Polo Grounds today to see the Red Sox play the Yankees, and he sat concealed behind Post 15 in the grandstand, totally incognito for nearly four seconds. Then the inmates of the pest-box smoked him out.

Pat had with him Grover Cleveland Alexander, who is to play the Red Sox for the world's championship the latter part of this week, and Grover brought Bill Killifer, his pig-tail in his important games. Grover and Bill remained more open and exposed than Pat throughout the afternoon. They are what you might call shameless about their presence.

Newspaper Men on Job

Between the first and second games Pat went down to the pest-box gate near the Sox bench and squatted on his haunches in the aisle, emitting cries for Bill Carrigan. Nineteen persons, or about 94 per cent of the total attendance, helped him out by lifting their voices, acting as messengers and generally making themselves useful and obnoxious.

Bill was finally located, and came over to the gate, and then and there the scene that should have been reserved for the world's series was pushed on. They shook hands. It was most impressive.

"Hello, Bill," said Pat.

"Hello, Pat," said Bill.

And little did they think that Old Ironsides, the International News Service photographer, at anchor lay in the oiling, snatching photographic reproductions of the imposing situation, while newspaper writers massed themselves close up and took notes of the conversation with frantic haste. We dislike gossip and scandal, but we must say that we have a feeling that but for one thing, Old Ironsides would not turn in those films at this time, but would hold 'em out to save himself work during the world's series, when he could send 'em marked, "Managers Moran and Carrigan shake hands as Sox and Phils hurl themselves into the fray."

The one thing that is going to prevent this chichany on Old Ironsides's part is the fact that Pat Moran was attired in plain clothes, while Bill Carrigan wore the livery of his calling. Even as desperate a character as Old Ironsides would never try to get away with that kind of film.

More "Conversation"

Resuming our report of the conversation between Pat and Bill, we find on reference to our notes that they spoke in part as follows:

"Hello, Bill,"

"Hello, Pat."

After that the conversation grew very conventional, and not worthwhile. We hear that Pat congratulated Bill, and Bill congratulated Pat, and then they went on.

"Well, good-by Pat," said Bill.

"Good-by, Bill," said Pat. "See you Friday."

"All right, Pat," said Bill.

It was certainly a great scene, with the newspaper boys all about and Old Ironsides snatching pictures, and the nineteen fans pressed in close, and everybody all worked up and everything, but somehow we feel that they have clouded the film for the world's series.

We saw a lot of persons interviewing G. Cleveland Alexander, who plays the Red Sox Friday, but we must confess we did not go near him. We were afraid he might say he is confident of beating the Sox, although they seem to have a good ball club, and that he is feeling simply grand, and can pitch three games if necessary, just like Jacob wrote the note. We were afraid that he might tell us that he is not entitled to all the credit he is getting for his great showing, and that his teammates are responsible for everything.

Fails to Interview Grover

We sorely feared he would start in to describe those teammates to us: their many lovable characteristics and their little kindnesses to the folks at home, and how they just went ahead and played steady ball behind him, and didn't hurrah the umpires more than necessary, and what a grand guy is Pat Moran. Oh, what a grand guy, and "Loody" and "Cravvy," and all the rest. And we just knew that we'd get to remarking in the paper about the intense modesty of this young bird who is the talk of the nation, and how he sat there so careless-like and loose in his seat, and tried so hard to avoid being interviewed that no one would ever have suspected that he was Alexander the Great.

Well, nobody did suspect at that, outside of everybody present, and there wasn't enough present to make the suspicion very general.

So, as we were saying, we did not interview Grover, but a lot of others did, and so what he said will not appear in numerous prints.

What he thought even is a very exclusive item with this paper. We hired a mind reader to go around and read Grover's mind during the afternoon; and so we are enabled to give an accurate report on the hurler's thoughts—that is, it is accurate unless the mind reader deceived us. The mind reader says he knows Grover was thinking that way, because everybody else was, and great minds run in the same channel.

"So this is the Boston bunch, is it?" thought "Alick." "The champions of the American League, and they are going to try to beat me out of a world's championship. Well! Well! It's a shame to receive the currency. Why, that fellow Leonard can't pitch up an alley, and this Histler or Croster or Foster, or whatever his name is, is just in there throwing the baseball. I suspect these are the Degnon Grays they're playing. Someone told me I'd get to see the Yanks and the Red Sox, but, of course, they've rung in the Degnon Grays as the Yanks. That's too bad, because I wanted to see the Yanks.

Mind Reader's Report

"If the Red Sox can't lick a semipro outfit, how are they going to lick us? And that's the great Speaker out there, is it? Well, he must have been putting on that muff he made of Nunamaker's knock. He had the ball right in his hands. Paskert would have held on. And Speaker'll be leaving his arm on the Polo Grounds if he tears off many more of those throws from the Harlem River to third.

"I hear they took Scott out and put Janvrin in because Scott was booting the ball around too much. Well, Bancroft won't boot many of 'em. We haven't had to take him out for that reason all season. So Scott boots 'em, does he? Well, I'll tell the boys to chunk 'em all at him. I don't think some of these birds would hit me with a board. And Moran down there handing Carrigan the old stuff. What are we over here for anyway? I've seen enough. Curve for that guy, curve for this one, curve, curve, curve, curve; but not so much speed, no. They love their speed. Not much speed for them Friday. Well, I wish I was back in dear old Philly."

Maybe the mind reader got his mental wires crossed and read the mind of Bill Fleishmann, but the above is what he turned in to us on "Alick." And, of course, "Alick" would never, never put such thoughts into words, even if he thunk 'em, for "Alick" is nothing if not a gent.

Same Old Alibi

Of course, the Sox had an alibi for their showing against the Yanks today. You can bet they had it. In the first place, they said the Sox don't beat the Yanks very much anyway, and in the second place, the Sox have been laying off for some days and need a few pastimes under their respective belts to put them in championship form, and the Yanks are not the Phillies. The alibi, like the poor, is always with us.

Not that we think the showing of the Sox today was any line on the form they will display in the world's series. Tris Speaker will not miss another fly such as he muffed today in the next ten years, and it was a difficult chance, too, while young Foster can pitch better ball with his left-hand than he showed today with his right.

It is very likely Carrigan will start Foster in the series, and this will be exercising good judgment. Foster is far and away the headiest pitcher on the Sox staff, though he may not have as much natural stuff as "Long" Shore. He is a cracking good pitcher, is Foster, and the workout today should put him right on edge.

Richmond Times-Dispatch
October 6, 1915

Mayer Looming Up Big

Damon Runyon Calls Attention To Pitcher

Believes That J. Erskine May Cause Boston Red Sox Trouble in Series

In 1914 J. Erskine Mayer won twenty-one games and lost nineteen for a sixth-place club over in Philadelphia. This season, up to the last accounting, he has won nineteen and lost fifteen pastimes for the championship outfit led by Pat Moran. Toss out J. Erskine's overhand work and where would Philadelphia's pennant be?

It is difficult to see how the experts can overlook J. Erskine in the ante-mortem statements. True, the loud cries over the exploits of G. Cleveland Alexander have drowned out nearly all other sound connected with the Philadelphia club, but even after they get through talking about Grover, you rarely hear the name of "Irksome" Mayer. They mention George Chalmers, the Harlem hurricane, ahead of Mayer and even Epha Jeptha Rixey, the well-known college cry, has been noticed before Erskine.

He May Cause Trouble

Mayer has not been going well of late, according to the men who follow the Phils, but the last time the club was in Brooklyn he seemed to be all right again and a pitcher with his record is not to be despised in a bear fight. Wild Bill Donovan, manager of the Yanks, made the statement some days ago that he would not be surprised if Mayer's underhand delivery did not cause the Red Sox a lot of trouble, basing his assertion on the showing that Jack Warhop used to make against the Boston club.

Mayer and Warhop have similar pitching styles, but Mayer has much more "stuff" on the ball than Jack. He is stronger physically and younger. He worked in forty-eight games in 1914 and in forty-one this year, up to the last edition of the records. George Chalmers has been making a strong finish, but George had none of Mayer's effectiveness early in the season, when Erskine and Alexander carried the club along.

Good left-handers bother the Red Sox, but Moran is practically all out of good left-handers. He has two left-handers all right, but neither has as yet produced records that qualify him for the good class.

Rixey as Sweeper-Up

Epha Jeptha Rixey, the elongated Virginia collegian, who was extracted from an educational institution a couple years ago by Charley Rigler, the National League umpire, is credited with eleven victories and eleven defeats in the averages which are before us. He figured in twenty-nine games in this past season. In 1914 he was out twenty-four times and produced just two wins against eleven defeats, showing that he was used chiefly as a sweeper-up of pastimes.

He has never stood out to any extent in point of ability among the left-handers of the National League. Now and then he would have a good day, but generally he was regarded as easy picking. Withal he displayed enough "stuff" to warrant the Philadelphia managers in carrying him along, and some day he may be a very great pitcher. He is one of the tallest men in the game, and drops the ball down on the batter from 'way, 'way up yonder. Some baseball men contend that a pitcher can be altogether too tall for effectiveness, but the average manager likes 'em just as tall as he can get 'em.

If the Sox give the Philadelphia right-handers a sound beating, Rixey will undoubtedly get his chance; but he will probably represent Moran's very last line of defense. Pat has another side-winder—young Baumgartner, but Baumgartner is not likely to be started. Neither is George McQuillan regarded as a possibility in the series, while Al Demaree would be another long shot. Alexander, Mayer and Alexander is the logical sequence of Pat's pitching experiments for the first three days at least, assuming that Alexander gets by in his opening start.

Philly Flingers Different

Even if he is defeated, "Alick" will unquestionably get another crack at the box, but this decisive defeat will mean a general shift in Moran's plans.

If you have ever paid any particular attention to the Philadelphia flingers, you must have noted that they have a style somewhat different from the pitchers of other clubs. At least the pitchers who might be called Philadelphia trained have this distinctive style, although Al Demaree and George McQuillan still pitch about the same as the average hurler.

Alexander, Mayer and Chalmers, however, all have a way of twisting their bodies in a wind-up so their backs are to the batters just before they swing around again to deliver the ball. Charley Dooin' inculcated this style in the pitchers, and ball players say it is responsible for much of Alexander's effectiveness.

That Charley was a good pitcher coach, whatever he may have lacked as a manager, is indicated by the present stars of the Philadelphia staff, but some managers do not like the back-to-the-batter method of delivery. However, it must be remembered that many managers do not care much for pitchers with the side-arm motion characteristic of Alexander.

"Alick" Is Still Going

Several of our acquaintances have had a hard time seeing Alexander at all for some years. They felt sure he would wear out with that motion, and yet "Alick" is going along about the same as ever.

That city series between the Giants and the Yanks is on after all, but New York is saved. The contest will not occur here. Hartford is the fall town. Hartford has stood for George Cohan's first productions and divers manifestations of Ol' Walt Trumbull, so it should be able to bear up nicely under the Yank-Giant thing.

It seems that the Elks of Hartford are staging a game between the two New York clubs, and Friday is the day selected. The Elks wish it distinctly understood however, that they did not pick this date with any intention of detracting from the opening of the world's series.

In order to get the Yanks tuned up for the Hartford matter the Red Sox have agreed to play another game in this city on Thursday. This will be the game that should have been played to-day, but has no reference to the two or more games which will be played to-morrow. The Red Sox will not play here on Friday because the world's series intervenes, but they may return for a few more games after the world's series just to make it a full season.

Washington Herald
October 8, 1915

Bleacher Fans Await Charge on the Gates

Army of Men and Boys Camping Out All Night in Rain for Choice Seats in New Stands.

Philly Baseball Mad

In easy striking distance of the dollar gates of the old baseball yard of the Philadelphia Nationals, at Huntington and Broad streets, a motley army of men and boys is bedded down tonight in packing cases filled with straw, or hunched up in convenient doorways, awaiting the charge upon the bleacher seats for the opening game of the world's series tomorrow.

A cold autumnal rain is laving the City of Brotherly Love. Dripping and chilled, and generally miserable, the campers of the night preserve the semblance of a line which stretches nearly all the way from Fifteenth street to Broad, on Lehigh Avenue. Here and there a woman is seen.

Downtown the hotel lobbies are packed with notables of the baseball world. On the sidewalks in front of every hostelry range hungry hordes of ticket speculators. Everywhere there is a hum of gossip—stories of ticket scandals; rumors of jobs against the local baseball magnates by the Philadelphia civic authorities and politicians; whispers of unsafe stands at the Philly field; and some talk of the baseball game that is scheduled for tomorrow.

It is not likely that the game will be played. The ball ground is soaked, and the weather prediction for tomorrow is more rain. Unless there is a strong blast of sunshine in the morning, the opening of the series will have to be postponed until Saturday. The wet line waiting out there at the ball park will have had its weary vigil for nothing.

Reminds One of 1911

The situation is strongly reminiscent of 1911, when the Giants were rained in here for a couple of days during the series with the Athletics, and when inertia developed the wildest kind of gossip and weird rumors. Give a baseball crowd twenty-four hours of idleness, and it will work up its own sensations without any vast effort.

The squawk of the exasperated Philadelphia fan fills the community this evening. The cramped yard of the Philadelphia club will seat about 21,000 people, and all the seats have been allotted save about 7,500 bleacher seats, which will be tossed to the waiting line at Broad and Huntington about 11 o' clock tomorrow morning. Old-time fans, followers of the Phils, who have been spending their money at the ancient ball yard year in and year out hoping almost against hope for the scene which will be enacted tomorrow, say they have been forgotten, and are unable to get tickets.

Yet tonight you could step out of the Bellevue Stratford Hotel into Broad Street and buy a brace of seats without any great trouble.

You could buy them. But you would have to pay as high as $40 for a set of pasteboards that have a face value of $9. These are the $3 seats. For the $2 seats the speculators modestly asked $25 to $30 per set.

Specs Trying to Buy

And, it is only fair to say that the speculators don't appear to be in possession of any considerable number of tickets. Most of them are trying to buy, rather than to sell. In other years when the Athletics were playing in the championship games, the "specs" would be lined up all along Broad street from the station to the Bellevue Stratford, and all were on sale. They generally had plenty of tickets, but tonight they sidle through the crowds crying offers to purchase.

The local police began chasing them away later, but they always bobbed up again, insistent and persistent.

Among the numerous rumors floating about today was one that the police had tried to "shake down" the Philadelphia management for a big bundle of tickets, threatening to withhold police protection if the tickets were not forthcoming, but the coppers seemed active enough tonight against the "specs."

As a matter of fact, the Philadelphia ball club had only about 12,000 tickets to give out. Of that number the national commission clutches 1,200 under some inalienable ball right which has ever been a deep mystery.

Washington Herald
October 9, 1915

Breaks Of Luck Are Big Factor

Gods of Fortune Smile on the Mighty Alexander in Phillies' Initial Victory Over Red Sox by 3 to 1.

Tough Lines For Shore

"Alec" did it. The gods of baseball fortune smiled very, very kindly on the big star of the Philadelphia Nationals and the men behind him, this afternoon, but he did what he was expected to do. He won.

He carried his club through to a 3 to 1 victory over the Boston Red Sox in the opening game of the world series. Slipping and slopping and staggering along, he carried it through, and though he must have gone to bed tonight with a feeling that Friday was a mighty auspicious day for Grover Cleveland Alexander, he won.

That's the main thing—he won.

The world pauses but briefly to analyze the reasons for a winner. It may sympathize a fleeting moment with Ernest Shore, the long, thin, scissors-legged lad from 'way down South in Georgia: he will hear a great deal the next few hours about his "tough luck," and then the procession will move on in the wake of Alexander, called The Great.

He won. Shore lost.

The Royal Rooters, of Boston, 400 strong, tramping disconsolately across the muddy field of the Phils behind their band and the only "Honey Fitz" late this afternoon, mumbled "horseshoes" at the shrilling thousands in the stand, but a hundred yards away Alexander was fighting his way toward the clubhouse door through a wild jam of humanity that chanted: "Oh, you Alec."

Alexander Gets Breaks

Pitching nothing like the mighty Alexander who shoved the heavy-footed Phillies across the summer months of the National League campaign, his delivery was cracked to all corners of the yard in eight sharp, decisive hits, while his towering young opponent was holding the clubbers of the Philadelphia outfit to five safe blows—four of them spongy infield rollers—the big Nebraskan had to have all of what baseball men call "the breaks" to win.

Tonight in the huge parlor of the Bellevue-Stratford Hotel that is used for press headquarters, above a weird jangle of typewriters rocking under the fingers of two score newspaper men telling the tale of the day's game, can be heard a hum of argument which indicates widely varying views of the proceedings.

"Scott's boner in the eighth did it," says a Boston man, irate over the defeat.

"Paskert's catch in the eighth saved the day," asserts a Philadelphian.

"All luck," declares an out-of-towner.

"Nothing but luck. Alexander had a rabbit's foot."

But the score remains unchanged—3 for Philadelphia and 1 for the Boston Red Sox.

Nothing Sensational

There was nothing Homeric about the struggle. Did it take place on any Friday in the run of the regular session, it would be called a poor game, a listless, draggy game, for in the regular session it would carry none of the interest that naturally centers about a world's championship fight.

There was just one flare of the spectacular in the course of the afternoon. That was George Paskert's catch in the eighth. Going into that inning the Phillies had a one-run lead. Scott, the young shortfielder whose error of omission later on rests heavily on the minds of the Boston rooters this evening, was retired on a fly to Bancroft.

Tris Speaker, the Texan, generally recognized as the greatest fielding outfielder in the baseball world, was given a base on balls by Alexander. The pitcher tried to "work the corners" on Tris, which translated means that he endeavored to put the ball over the edge of the plate farthest from the Lone Star slugger.

Something should be said here of the craft displayed by Alexander in working on the Boston batsmen.

Alexander a Little Wild

Maybe it was overcaution in this respect that made him a little wild. Maybe it was extreme care that was responsible for what the baseball people are now calling "ragged" pitching. He had passed Speaker in the first inning trying to confine his delivery to a scant few inches of the plate, and now, in this eighth, he did not get a ball across that William Klem, shrill-voiced, dapper, alert, umpiring behind the bat, could call a strike.

As craftily as Alex worked, just as craftily did Speaker squat there, sliding his eyes along the range where he knew the ball must come to suit his purpose. The great Texan is growing gray in the service of the Sox, but no pitcher, however wonderful, may take liberties with him.

He walked. Dick Hoblitzel, discard of the Cincinnati Reds, and passed up by every club in the National League, only to find himself in a world series, hit a sharp grounder down to Milton Stock, the pudgy little third baseman discovered and developed by John J. McGraw, of the Giants, to finally make a useful player for another manager.

Stock Makes Fumble

Stock fumbled the ball for an instant. But for that fumble he might have had a chance to toss the ball of Bert Neihoff at second and start a double play. Seeing it was too late to get Speaker at second, however, the small Chicagoan twirled the ball over to Luderus and Hoblitzel was called out by "Silk" O'Loughlin, the American League umpire, in that high vocal scream that carries to the distant edges of a crowd.

Duffy Lewis slugged the first ball pitched at him by Alexander for a single to left field. Speaker was in motion with the swing. He crossed the plate several feet ahead of George Whitted's arm, and though Burns whipped the ball down to Neihoff as soon as he saw he could not tag Speaker, the Californian was easily safe.

Then it was that Larry Gardner drove a fly far out over center field, but a little toward left, and then it was that Paskert came racing up out of the distance and clutched the ball while traveling at full speed. That catch may have changed the entire aspect of the game. Had the drive gone safe the Sox would have been in front. The things that occurred in the Phillies' end of the same inning might not have been.

Shore Unsteady

And that would have relieved poor little Scott of a lot of criticism that is not altogether just. Maybe, too, a Sox advantage might have held the gawky Shore steady. Fresh from a little school down South, Shore joined the Giants a couple of years back, as green in point of baseball experience as the greens come. He was put into the last inning of a game against the Boston Braves in which the Giants had a huge lead, and was hit for ten runs, though the Giants won out.

After that Shore got homesick for the South. He wanted to go back to college and McGraw finally let him go, giving him an unconditional release. Later Jack Dunn, of the Baltimore Orioles, picked him up and developed him and sold him for a fat price to the Red Sox. It was that same Shore who faced the Phillies today as the star of the Boston staff, and that same Shore who pitched well against the champions of the National League today.

Alexander was the first man to bat in the eighth, and he was thrown out by Black Jack Barry, once shortstop of the great Athletic machine, but now second baseman of another championship outfit. Great was Black Jack Barry today. Stock waited on Shore until he drew a base on balls, although the Georgian managed to mix in a brace of strikes. Shore was getting unsteady even now. Bancroft smashed a grounder across second. It seemed impossible that any infielder in the world could get that skipping ball, but "Black Jack" performed the impossible.

Makes Good Catch

He tore over well back of second and got the drive with one hand. Had Scott been covering second as he should have been when he saw Barry after the ball, and Stock racing for the middle bag, the latter would have been an easy out, but Scott was at his usual position, and, apparently, as much surprised by Barry's wonderful play as anybody in the crowd. "Black Jack" came up with the ball in his bare hand and started to snap it to second, when he saw Scott was not there. In an instant Scott dashed over to the sack, and then Barry made the throw, but it was too late. Stock flung his pudgy body in under Scott's stab and was safe.

It was a close play. It would have been one of the most remarkable plays ever seen on a ball field had it gone through, but no one murmured over "Silk" O'Loughlin's decision.

Washington Herald
October 11, 1915

Alexander The Hope Of Phils

Quakers Are Depending on Big Nebraskan to Bring Home Bacon Today

Expect Record Crowd

The hope of Philadelphia in this current world series, which is engaged at present in commuting on the New York, New Haven, and Hartford, grows. It grew at least four pounds tonight.

The hope of Philadelphia weighed in at about 185 pounds on the O'Sullivan at 6 p.m. and approximately 189 pounds an hour later when the inhalation of a sirloin steak and accessories had been completed. After which the hope of Philadelphia slipped the waiter the conventional dime, secured a toothpick and went out in front of the Copley Square Hotel to see what could be seen.

In mentioning the hope of Philadelphia in the world series we refer, of course, to Grover Cleveland Alexander, alias The Great. If Philadelphia has any other hope in this world series, it isn't discernible to the naked eye. Not at present writing, anyway—not right this very minute.

A man goes a mighty long way to be a hope when he goes from St. Paul, Nebr., to Broad and Huntington streets, but that's the present status of G. C. Alexander.

He's a hope—no, not a hope, either: but THE hope. Tomorrow afternoon Mr. Alexander resumes active operations in the hoping business at the large, airy and commodious ballyard of the Boston Braves, with the Boston Red Sox as his opponents. The rest of the Philadelphia ball club is at the Copley Square Hotel with Grover, but no matter. The Philadelphia ball club is batting only .158 in this series, so Grover can scarcely expect any assistance from it.

Expect 45,000 Fans

The yard of the Boston Braves holds something like 45,000 people, and there will be that many present at the game tomorrow. It is the first game of the series to be played in Boston, and with the clubs standing fifty-fifty at this time, the haunt of the wild baked bean and the mad-broiled scrod finds itself genteely agitated.

Not that a world series is any novelty to Boston—not at all. The old cradle of the National League has been rocked by so many baseball sensations of late years that it is almost blase, but the idea of getting into some place where a lot of other people won't be able to get into somehow appeals to the Boston imagination. And then here is the prospect of seeing Grover Cleveland Alexander, who is of more local interest at this moment than the Bunker Hill Monument or Percy Haughton.

Among the 45,000 spectators tomorrow will be all the prominent people of Fitchburg, which gave Pat Moran, the Old Junkman, to the world's series cause. Several reserved seats have been set aside for them, and they are going to root for Patrick—not that they hate Boston, but because they love Patrick more.

Bill Must Pick Hurler

The old Junkman has one advantage tonight over his loathed enemy, Bill Carrigan—Pat doesn't have to worry about what pitcher he should work tomorrow, as he made his selection for this game the day he won the pennant in the National League. If he hadn't made his selection then, the experts would have made it for him, so what's the difference?

The experts have been mighty obliging in this series, picking the battery for the manager, and everything, but Pat crossed most of them yesterday when he nominated J. "Irksome" Mayer.

It is with no little pride that we call attention to the fact that we said Pat would work "Irksome" and hinted "Irk" might pitch surprisingly well; we are proud of that because it was the first time we have been right in connection with a world series since

Abraham Lincoln was assassinated. However, we view with some alarm the possibility that Pat may cross us and not work "Aleck" tomorrow.

It seems unlikely, but anything is possible in this series. It is even possible for Bert Niehoff to get himself one and no one hundreds' safe blow. George Chalmers, the Harlem Hurricane, is hanging around in the Philadelphia offing, and it requires no great stretch of the imagination to see Pat growing reckless and starting George.

Pat Will Play His Ace

But we think not. Not tomorrow at all events. When a man, sound in mind and perfectly sober, holds an ace, he generally leads that ace. If Alexander can best the Sox again tomorrow, the Phillies will have the boys two down and two to go, and Chalmers or Mayer can space out Tuesday, leaving G. Cleveland for Wednesday and maybe Thursday.

But if the Sox beat Alexander tomorrow—oh, well, we'd just as soon go back to New York direct as by way of Philadelphia.

The experts are commencing to like this series. They like it because it is running true to form. At least it is running true to form up to the present. They all said Philadelphia had just one pitching chance for victory—and Philadelphia still has it. It is difficult to see how a .158 batting average can hope to overwhelm a pounding mark of .261, but Alexander may do it.

Among American League baseball men, the showing of George Foster in Philadelphia yesterday was by no means surprising, as they regard the blocky young right-hander as one of the best pitchers in the game. Only a few days before the series began, Wild Bill Donovan, manger of the Yankees, expressed the belief that Foster would give the Phillies a great deal of trouble.

Foster a Sensation

In fact, it was the opinion of the baseball world that Carrigan would start the series with Foster instead of Shore, because while Foster may not have the same amount of natural stuff as the

Georgian, he is a smarter pitcher, and has more experience. He is a fellow somewhat on the order of Rudolph, of the Braves, but Rudolph no longer possesses anything like Foster's speed and curves.

The New York Giants ran against Foster a couple of years ago at Houston, in the Texas League, and Foster blanked the McGraw regulars in an exhibition game. He was then about the best pitcher the Giants had encountered in a spring time exhibition in years, and his feat caused no little comment among the ball players.

Boston fans are firmly convinced that if Carrigan handles his pitchers right, the rest of the series is a walkaway. Many believe that a repeat with Shore tomorrow would be the logical course, in view of the way Shore was outlucked in the opener by Alexander, but it is more than likely that Carrigan will try one of his lefthanders—"Dutch" Leonard, or "Babe" Ruth—first, and hold Shore over for Tuesday. He can then use Foster again on the return to Philadelphia.

Jake Stahl made one serious mistake with his pitchers in 1912, when the Boston Red Sox had the Giants on the run, by putting in Bucky O'Brien, the spitballer, in the sixth game. Joe Wood was the logical starter, and Stahl's course in using O'Brien is said to have caused a big row in the ranks. A balk by Bucky upset the Red Sox, and the Giants won easily.

True, Wood was given a terrific pasting in the next game, but conditions had changed, and, anyway, that did not alter the fact that Stahl should have tried Joe in his logical sequence.

Washington Herald
October 12, 1915

Scott's Sacrifice Is A Big Factor

Youthful Shortfielder of Carrigan's Sox Gives Boston Chance to Win Game

Duffy Lewis Real Hero

Timely Clout After Speaker Had Been Passed Spelt Defeat For the Great Alexander and Phillies

By a crook of his finger: by the careless flipping of a clod—whatever his code may be—Bill Carrigan, manager of the Boston Red Sox, flashed a brief instruction in the wireless, wordless language of the ball field to Everett Scott, his young shortfielder, in the ninth inning of the third game of the world series, and a few moments later Alexander, called The Great, had fallen.

That sign of Carrigan's produced the only real baseball strategy that has been used in this series. It brought about the defeat of the Phillies by a score of 2 to 1. It was the play that definitely turned the flank of the mighty Alexander. It was the play that started the rout of the Phillies, but it was not the play that set 43,000 people packed in the stands and bleachers to roaring.

It was the play that the so-called experts of baseball will expatiate of at length, but the play that brought the crowd up standing, and filled the field with a great volume of noise, was when Duffy Lewis, the chunky Californian veteran of many a desperate diamond tussel, smashed a single to centerfield, with Harry Hooper, another native son of the Golden West, poised on third, and Tris Speaker, the great Texan, intentionally passed for safety's sake by Alexander, jockeying around second.

Two were out and the score was tied when Lewis came to the plate, swishing a long bat as lightly as if it were a toothpick. One ball was pitched to him by Alexander—fairly high, and smoking fast—and there followed baseball stories. There came an instant's hush, all eyes trailed the whirling ball, and presently the strains of "Tessie," war song of Boston's Royal Rooters, spilled along the field behind the band and the high hat of "Honey Fitz."

Lewis Soaked the Pill

That one ball pitched to Lewis by Alexander is causing many a heated argument tonight. It brings up many an angle of the technique and the science of the baseball field, incoherent enough to the mind of the layman, which understands only that Duffy soaked that pill and won that ball game. It comprehends no mistake in pitching judgment about that smash; it sees no room for chance in a hit by a man who had already made two hits—half of the total number acquired by the Sox from the thunderbolt pitching of Alexander.

If it sees any mistakes, it probably sees only the mistakes of the Phillies, including the great Alexander himself, when they lost two distinct chances to win the game before they were irretrievably enmeshed in the impenetrable left hand of Dutch Leonard.

And maybe the lay mind will have some difficulty in compassing the strategy of the play that really won the game—the play that goes back beyond the one ball pitched to Lewis by Alexander, which baseball men say was such a grievous blunder, but we shall tell of that play as it occurred, and explain it as it is explained by the sages of the national game.

Harry Hooper opened the last half of the ninth inning with a line drive to right, which went as a single. The shrill voice of "Silk" O'Loughlin, the American League umpire, working behind the plate, had tolled off a strike, and then Hooper fouled off the second and third pitches before he slugged the ball to the territory patrolled by old "Wooden Shoes" Cravath.

Brings Infield In

The next play logical for the Sox under the circumstances, was a bunt to advance Hooper. As young Scott stepped to the plate, he had his bat hugged close to his crest, his hands gripped the stick in the middle—"chocked" as the ball players call it. The Phillies' infield moved in toward the plate—the stolid Luderus, who fanned three times today before the left-handed sweeps of "Dutch" Leonard; the quiet Nichoff, Bancroft; the sensational, and the pudgy-legged, chattering Stock.

Scott pushed his bat stiffly at the first ball pitched, and fouled it off. As he moved the Philly infielders rushed forward, hawk-like expectant, then fell back a trifle, as Alexander swung his arm, and Scott again crouched in a hitting posture. The infield moved up once more with the lashing of Alexander's arm, and again Scott fouled the ball with the awkward bunting motion that is designed to just drop the ball a few inches in front of the plate.

That made two strikes on Scott, and under these circumstances the ordinary proceeding would have been for him to abandon the attempt to bunt and take his full swing at the ball, trying for a safe hit. If he failed to hit the ball on a third attempt at bunting he would be out under the rules.

The Philadelphia infield evidently expected a swing as it fell back to the usual positions. Scott no longer held himself tense at the plate: his body was relaxed and he had the attitude of a man about to "take his Moriarity," as the ball players say, meaning a healthy swing. But the sign had reached him from Carrigan and at the next ball he reached out his bat and deftly caught the ball with a light snap.

It was harder than he intended: it was so hard that it carried the ball out past Alexander to Niehoff, as Niehoff came rushing in, after wasting an instant to get started, but it was sufficient to advance Hooper to second while Niehoff was throwing out Scott at first, and it was sufficient to totally unravel the frayed nerves of the Philadelphia club.

It had been a hard enough strain as it was, holding back the rushing Sox, even behind the superb catching of Alexander.

It brought Tris Speaker to bat and scored the tying run for the Sox, in the fourth inning, his own triple to right field, and Hoblitzel's sacrifice. Tris came up swinging three bats, to make the one he retained feel lighter in his hand, a fashion inaugurated by Ty Cobb.

"I can stand for the boys swinging two bats," remarked Bill Lange, the Ty Cobb of his time who sat in the press box, "but three seems to me a good many bats."

Without any consultation whatever; with the manner of carrying out a plan arranged long before, little "Eddie" Burns stepped well to one end of the catcher's box, and Alexander began throwing the ball wide of the plate, intentionally giving Speaker his base on balls.

The Boston fans jeered derisively. "Tessie" came rolling out of the cavernous depths of the single-decked stand, erected by the owners of the Boston Braves after they won the world's championship, and donated for this occasion to the manager of the Sox, on whose field the Braves crushed the Athletics a year ago.

As Speaker trotted to first, apparently somewhat surprised, Alexander faced to Dock Hoblitzel, the National League discard. The big sidearmer worked on as little of the plate as possible for Hobby, and soon the count was three balls and no strikes and even the Philadelphia fans felt that trouble was coming. Hoblitzel finally hit a grounder to Niehoff and Niehoff tossed the ball to Luderus for the second out, but Hooper and Speaker advanced to second and third, respectively, and Lewis was at bat.

Some argue that, in view of Lewis' previous two hits, it would have been good policy to pass him, but then Larry Gardner, who followed him in the batting order, is almost as dangerous. All baseball men seem to agree, however, that Alexander used poor judgment in putting that first ball where he did. It may be that the Nebraskan tried to "slip one over" on Lewis or that he hardly expected Duffy to hit at the first ball, but the course of the Sox throughout the earlier part of the game renders this theory untenable.

Both runners could have scored easily on Lewis' smash had it been necessary. Paskert picked up the ball and made no attempt to throw it. Hooper was over the plate when the outfielder got the ball, and the fast Speaker was rounding third. Even a creasing line throw would not have caught the Texan.

The whole Philadelphia club stood motionless for almost a minute while the crowd began swarming on the field to surround the triumphant Sox, and then they came gloomily marching in, to be lost in the swirling throng.

No Philadelphia player got to first on Leonard after the third, but between the first and the third the Phillies lost two great opportunities.

The attendance today broke all records for paid attendance at a professional ball game. The high-water mark was reached in New York some years ago with 38,000, and that was at a world series game. In Boston, on Labor Day last year, about 70,000 people saw the national pastime, but they were divided into morning and afternoon crowds. There were no temporary bleachers erected today, and along the end of the right field bleachers several thousand fans were standing.

Washington Herald
October 13, 1915

Lewis Comes Through Again in the Pinch

Foxy George Chalmers, of Pat Moran's Phillies, Tries to Slip One Past Boston Outfielder—Result, Timely Hit and Winning Run of Brilliant 2 to 1 Victory

There will probably never be much of an argument as to the nature of the third ball pitched at Duffy Lewis, citizen of Boyes Hot Springs, Sonoma County, Cal., by George Chalmers, the "Harlem Hurricane," in the sixth inning of the fourth game of the world series this afternoon.

Yesterday, in the ninth inning, Grover Cleveland Alexander flung one ball at the chunky leftfielder of the Boston Red Sox and Duffy broke up the game on the Philadelphia's star.

Whereat the baseball world chattered wildly. Alexander was careless, they said. Alexander had put the ball right in Lewis' "groove." "Alexander should have 'worked' his man more. Alexander should not have given him a good ball to hit. It was a waist-high curve that he threw. It was a high fast one. It was a low twister. But whatever it was, it wasn't right. And so on, and so on, all night long around the hotel lobbies of Boston and through several columns of the morning papers.

Today George Chalmers, a canny Scot, pitching the wisest baseball shown by any Philadelphia hurler in this series, slipped two strikes over the plate on Lewis in the sixth and then tried another. Baseball history will record that the Red Sox won this game by a score of 2 to 1.

Outguessing the crafty Chalmers with rare judgment, Lewis slammed a two-bagger to leftfield, scoring Dick Hoblitzel with what proved to be the winning run. Hoblitzel had singled after the great Speaker had been retired.

Two Strikes Called

Lewis did not offer at the first two balls thrown his way by Chalmers. He stood quietly at the plate, rippling his long bat through the air, while Billy Evans, the immaculate umpire from the American League, lifted his right arm twice in quick succession to indicate the strikes.

An ordinary pitcher might have "wasted" the next ball—might have pitched it wide of the plate, but George Chalmers was no ordinary pitcher today. The Scot-born, Harlem-raised hurler of the Phillies was generally pronounced one of the safest men who ever mounted a mound so far as his work this afternoon was concerned, an opinion that might be used to point out the future quirks in the mental attitude of baseball people.

Alexander yesterday might have been trying to sneak one over on Lewis when he laid that first ball on top of the plate, and he was criticized for his pains. Today Chalmers did substantially the same thing, and it is called smart pitching. He tried to "cross" Lewis, but was outguessed.

The clout of the Californian puts the Boston Red Sox in a fair way to the greatest financial reward ever reaped by ball players in a championship contest of this nature. They had a one-run lead when Lewis drove in Hoblitzel in the sixth, but in the eight old "Wooden Shoes" Cravath, the home-run hitter who had been sadly handicapped by the wide area of outfield at the Braves' new yard, and by the distant fences, got a lucky triple, and scored on Luderus' third hit.

Luderus Leads Phils

Yesterday the only left-handed hitter on the Philadelphia team—Luderus—hung helpless at the plate before the side arm sweep of "Dutch" Leonard, striking out three times. Today he was the hitting star of the Phillies against the long drop of Ernest Shore, the Georgia boy.

Cravath has hit two or three "Philadelphia home runs" in the two games on the Boston field—blows that would have lifted the balls into the seats or over the wall of the little old bandbox at Broad and Huntington streets, but which here were easy ones for the wide ranging outfielders of the Boston Sox.

Today, in the eighth, after two were out, the big walloper smashed a drive that fell in front of Tris Speaker, generally accounted the most accurate fielder in the country, especially on ground balls.

He should have held it to a single, but the ball bounded over his head and rolled away back into deep center field, while Cravath rushed around to third. Luderus' drive went also in Speaker's direction and the Texan had trouble gauging this one too, only a fast recovery and a good throw to the infield held Luderus to first.

Dugey Steals Second

Little Dugey, substitute infielder of the Phillies, ran for the heavy footed Milwaukee mauler, and stole second on the second ball pitched by Shore at George Whitted. Immediately afterward Whitted hit an easy roller to Shore and then and there passed the last chance of the Phillies in the game and perhaps their last chance in the series.

The next game will be played tomorrow at Philadelphia, and Pat Moran will probably call on Grover Cleveland Alexander to lead the forlorn hope.

There is little doubt among baseball people tonight as to the final outcome of the series.

The scores of the various games indicate nothing of the disparity between the two teams. The Boston club is probably a much better club than it has shown, but it sometimes happens that when a champion fighter is pitted against a poor opponent the opponent counts so bad as to make the champion look bad. And maybe that same thing can happen in baseball.

Marked by Bad Baseball

From start to finish this series has been colorless: almost devoid of feature. It has been marked by bad baseball on both sides. The Phillies may be one of what some writer last season characterized as eight second-division clubs trying to win the National League pennant, but even they have displayed better ball than they have shown against the American League champions.

They have seemed afraid to cut loose and try anything bordering on the chance-taking in this series.

Today George Chalmers gave them a masterly pitching effort, but they could not, in return, give the lad from the old Seventeenth assembly district more than one run. Ernie Shore pitched fairly well, but Ernie Shore had the Phillies in front of him. Chalmers was facing the Red Sox. There is a difference.

Shore and Chalmers are both on the rejected list of the New York Giants. Shore was turned away as a raw recruit and Chalmers as a veteran who was trying to do a comeback. Chalmers is subject to rheumatism in the shoulder muscles, and his arm went back on him when he was with the Phillies a year or so ago.

He was given his release, and last spring John J. McGraw took him South with the Giants, as a free agent, but with some tacit understanding that if Chalmers' arm recovered he would be signed by the New York club. The spit-baller trained for several weeks at Marlin, and then went North with the Giants' second team, and acting in the dual capacity of pitcher for the Colts and correspondent for the New York sporting pages.

He did not show enough to get a Giant contract, and one day last spring George Wiltse, the old New York pitcher, who was managing Jersey City, went up to the Polo Grounds to sign Chalmers for that club. That same day Pat Moran came into town short of pitchers and agreed to give Chalmers one more chance. Chalmers promised Wiltse if he failed to make good with the Phillies he would sign with Jersey City. He blanked the Giants that afternoon.

He had indifferent success with the Phillies throughout the greater part of the season, but toward the close of the campaign he was doing grand work, and this afternoon against the sluggers of the Sox stood out like a champion. He seemed to be bothered by his old trouble at times, as he gripped his left hand around his right arm, and grimaced with pain, but he gave a game exhibition all the way. Time and again the huge crowd applauded his work.

Sixty thousand rushed the gates of the Braves' field this afternoon, and of that number over 15,000 went away. Oddly enough, the inside yard was not as large by at least 1,200 people as it was on the opening day in Boston. This was because the spectators were not allowed to stand in the rear of the seats as they were the day before.

It was Columbus Day, and Columbus Day is a holiday in Boston. There was a terrific jam at the entrances to the ball yard, and mounted policemen had to keep rushing their horses into the crush of humanity to clear pathways for the ticketholders. The weather was like midsummer and much too hot for the wraps carried by nearly all the spectators. It was baseball weather, right enough, but not Boston October weather.

The Boston royal rooters and their band with the inevitable "Tessie"; innumberable song "pluggers" equipped with megaphones; gay parties of chorus girls from the various shows playing in Boston; and an array of Scotch musicians in kilts lent a touch of color to the proceedings before the start of the game.

At the close of the sixth inning the band played "The Star Spangled Banner" and the 40,000 people present stood with bared heads. Even the ball players out in the field paused in their play, took off their caps and stood at attention.

The Sox got their first run in the third inning through one of the three bases on balls given by Chalmers. The spitballer worked "Black Jack" Barry down to a count of three balls and two strikes, and then passed him. Big Forest Cady bunted and Chalmers fell as he threw himself at the ball.

Even so, the pitcher might have tossed out Cady at first had Luderus remained on the bag, or had Niehoff gone in behind

Luderus to cover, but Luderus was rushing up to get the bunt, while Niehoff was also lunging in. As a result neither Barry or Cady were put out. Cady got credit for an infield single.

A moment later the Sox raised a cry of balk as Chalmers stepped out of the box after resuming his pitching position. Billy Evans nodded and Barry and Cady started to move forward, but Chalmers vociferously denied that he was on the rubber in the pitching position as defined by the rules and Evans asked Charley Rigler, the National League umpire, who was working on the bases, for his opinion.

Rigler upheld Chalmers and the runners were sent back. There was a consultation between Chalmers and Burns, and Shore then bunted to Stock. The third baseman was darting back to cover third when the ball was hit, the Sox base runners having got in motion, and the bunt caught him unprepared to make a quick play.

He managed to field the ball over to first ahead of Shore, but with a runner on third and another on second Hooper hit a roller back of the box which Niehoff missed after a flying leap, and Barry scored. Cady took third, but Scott fouled to Whitted, down the left field line, and Whitted came running back into the infield clutching the ball, and holding the base runners to their station.

Chalmers tried two pitch outs on Speaker, looking for a double steal, and then the next was a ball. Chalmers put his hands on his hips and stared at Evans on this decision. Eventually Speaker grounded to Luderus at first.

Most of the Phillies' opportunities have developed in the early innings of the games, and the game today was no exception. Stock opened the first inning with a single, and tried to stretch it into a double and was out at second.

Pat Moran was coaching off first at the time. Maybe he told Stock to keep moving in spite of the fact that Lewis, a great thrower, was right on top of the ball as Stock was rounding first, and maybe Stock did not hear what Moran said to him, for Stock is slightly deaf. In any event, he was out, and a moment later Bancroft walked. Had Stock held to first it would have put runners on first and second with no one cut, and perhaps changed the course of the inning.

Bancroft stole second, Barry dropping a good throw from Cady, and Paskert fanned and so did Cravath. While Shore was pitching to Paskert the Philly players called on Evans to examine the ball, and the umpire did so. Shore has been accused of using the forbidden emery ball, though there is probably nothing in the accusation.

In the second Luderus singled and the Philly strategists staged the old cut and dried bunt sacrifice which has become such a regular feature of the game. Whitted advanced Luderus all right and Niehoff promptly fouled to Cady. Burns was walked—apparently intentionally—and Chalmers fanned. Never does the Philadelphia club pull a play that is not anticipated by the opposition.

Niehoff walked in the fourth, with two out, and Burns singled, but that again brought Chalmers up, and while Chalmers rapped the ball hard, he merely succeeded in forcing Niehoff at third on a good play by Scott to Gardner.

In the eighth, with one out, Speaker almost knocked Stock over with a smash and took third on Hoblitzel's third hit. Lewis was intentionally passed by Chalmers, filling the bases. Gardener hit to Chalmers, who threw the ball to Burns, forcing out Speaker at the plate, while Burns relayed the ball to Luderus, doubling up Gardner.

Washington Herald
October 14, 1915

Native Sons of the Golden West Make Clouts Giving Sox Series

Harry Hooper Drives Ball Into Bleachers in Ninth Inning, Defeating Moran's Phillies, 5 to 4

Erskine Mayer Pounded

As a sort of doxology for the world series of 1915 nothing could be more appropriate than that ditty which begins:

"Oh, you old Pacific Coast,
Oh, you land I love the most."

The native sons of the Golden West, who have permeated the baseball championship contest from the start, finally ruined the whole affair this afternoon for Philadelphia, Pa.

It is certainly mighty fitting that they are now going to take Duffy Lewis and Harry Hooper out to the San Francisco Exposition in official form, so to speak, to exhibit them to their home folks, along with the rest of the Boston Red Sox—tonight the new champions of the baseball world.

In the ninth inning of the fifth game of the series this afternoon Hooper knocked the title far out of reach of the Philadelphia Nationals by shoving a home run into the center field bleachers, and with that same Dicker of his bat the Californian spilled at least $80,000 from the clutch of the baseball magnates, for another game with Boston would have meant that much.

Hooper Makes Clout

The score was tied and one was out when Hooper stepped to the plate. His drive made the final count 5 to 4. It was Hooper's second home run of the day, and the fourth home run of the game, and that other deadly product of the Land of the Setting Sun, Duffy Lewis—"Devil Duff"—whacked out one of the four.

Under the circumstances, it would not be out of place for the exposition authorities out there in California to set aside a native son home run day in honor of Messrs. Lewis and Hooper. "Devil Duff's" drive came in the eighth with a man on first, and put the Red Sox on even terms with the Phillies at a moment when the baseball people were rather gloomily contemplating another night ride to Boston.

Lewis' blow came in the wake of an infield hit secured by Del Gainer, the first man up in the eighth, and was a solid smash to the center field seats. Gainer, former member of the Detroit Tigers, had taken Dick Hoblitzel's place at first base when Pat Moran put in a left-handed pitcher to succeed Erskine Mayer, and his hit took the form of a slow roller down to Milton Stock, who let the ball play him a bit, instead of playing the ball. Gainer easily outstepped the throw.

Hits Into Bleachers

Then Lewis came up, let one ball pass him, listened indifferently to Bill Klem intone a strike, and then put his bat and body behind the next pitch. The twenty thousand Philadelphians gathered in the stand had been eyeing the Californian with considerable apprehension whenever he came to bat, remembering his deeds during the past few days, and a groan swept the stands and bleachers as the ball rose high, and sped far.

Eppa Jeptha Rixey, the young six-foot-five son of Old Virginia, a discovery of Umpire Charley Rigler, and a scion of a very distinguished family, was pitching at the time. Erskine Mayer, who made a good showing in the second game with his underhanded delivery, had started, but was removed in the third after Hooper hit his first homer into the bleachers, and Speaker singled to right.

Pat Moran will probably come in for a great deal of criticism because of his choice of pitchers. Grover Cleveland Alexander was warming up with Mayer in front of the Philadelphia bench before the game started, and it was generally believed that Moran would surely start the big Nebraskan. However, it was noted that the Old Junkman himself had on a catcher's mitt and was working with Mayer during the warming up and it may be that he thought Mayer displayed the most "stuff," that he looked the best.

Saving Alexander

It may be, too, that Moran figured if he could win today he would have Alexander to come back at the Sox himself, but whatever his idea, his failure to have his star lead the forlorn hope will long be remembered in Philadelphia. Toward the last Alexander was again on the sidelines warming up, while there was a great flutter in the "bull pen," where the pitchers get ready for a game, down by the left field bleachers, as Al Demaree and George McQuillan unlimbered their arms, but before Moran could make any contemplated change the Philadelphia cause was lost.

From the third to the eighth Rixey pitched well, the sudden shift from the right-handed pitching they have been getting throughout the series to a left-handed delivery which drove the ball with great speed across their chests bothered the left-handed batsmen of the Sox for a time. Harry Hooper is left-handed and a light hitter during the season against almost any kind of pitching, and on the first two balls delivered to him by Rixey in the ninth today he looked almost foolish. Both were strikes. He swung at one and the other was called.

Foster Strikes Out

George Foster, the Oklahoma boy who hurled his second victory of the series for the Sox, and who had established a reputation as a hitter, had preceded Hooper with a strike-out, and a murmur of admiration over the pitching of the gigantic young left-hander was passing over the stands when Hooper swung for the third time. The ball passed on a line to deep center, then struck the ground and bounded into the bleachers, almost hitting a policeman who sat on a soap box in front of the bleacher crowd. The copper ducked just in time to escape getting struck on the head by the hopping ball.

There went a young fortune for the baseball magnates, and there went something like $1,200 for each of the Philadelphia players.

It seems a scurvy trick of fate that the short field, which was supposed the thing that would be of tremendous help to the Phillies in the series, was the very thing that brought about their downfall. They did all their heaviest hitting in Boston on the wide field of the Braves, where the fleet-footed rangers of the Sox outfield were at their best, while here on their home grounds, where they have long been the terror of opposing National League pitchers on account of their penchant for pounding the ball over the walls, they were almost helpless.

Luderus Makes Homer

Fred Luderas, the Milwaukee mauler, put the Phillies back into the fight for the championship in the fourth inning today when he slammed a ball over the high right field fence with a man on the base line. Eppa Jeptha Rixey, the Virginian, tried to keep them in it, but before the clouting native sons of the Golden West there could be no holding ground.

Had old "Wooden Shoes" Cravath, home run king of the baseball world this past season, slugged the ball here today as he slugged it over in Boston, he would tonight be the hero of the occasion. Instead he fanned twice, and was a weakling in a notable pinch. It is doubtful if Luderus' blow today would have been a home run on the Boston field, but it was none the less a mighty wallop, and was one of the things that makes the Milwaukee man the Philadelphia star of the series.

The Bostons won three of the four victories in the series in the ninth inning. There was no department in which they did not outclass the Phillies, but their outfielders carried the burden of the battle. Lewis, Speaker and Hooper—it is an outfield combination that will long be remembered in baseball. The pitching of Foster was nothing exceptional today—in fact, it was very ordinary, and so was the pitching of Shore the day before, but the crushing attack of the Sox triumvirate requires only a light cover of curves.

Phillies Get Jump

The Phillies got away to a great start this afternoon. In the opening inning Foster hit Stock with the second ball pitched and Bancroft singled after making one attempt at the old moss-grown bunt that has been the despair of the Philly followers in the series. Paskert, whose outfielding work has been at least one bright feature to be recalled of the Philadelphia fight, bunted at Gardner, who knocked Hoblitzel spinning as he crossed ahead of Gardner's throw.

"Silk" O'Loughlin called Paskert safe, and then there was the first semblance of a squabble produced by the staid, unemotional series. The Sox players gathered about "Silk" and complained of Paskert, but O'Loughlin finally waved them away. Down in the bullpen "Babe" Ruth, the left-hander, and "Smoky Joe" Wood began warming up.

Cravath rolled to Foster, after taking one wild swing, and Foster threw to Thomas, retiring Stock at the plate. Thomas flung the ball to Hoblitzel, doubling up the slow-moving Cravath.

The other runners moved along, and then Luderus—pronounced "Loo-der-us," with the second syllable accented, took two lusty swings before landing on the ball for a double to left, which scored Bancroft and Paskert. The ball fell well beyond Lewis' outstretched hand and gave the Philadelphia people their first chance to cheer a little.

The Boston folks were so confident that the series would end today that the Royal Rooters did not accompany the club to Philadelphia—at least not in organized form. "Tessie" was not to be heard on the field, probably for the first time that a Boston club has been involved in a world series since back in 1903.

Following Luderus' clout Whitted raised a fly to Speaker and ended the first inning.

In the Sox's end of the second, with two out, Larry Gardner tripled to center. The Philly infielders closed in around Mayer for a consultation and the Sox trainer ran out to third and hastily stitched a rip in the knee of Gardner's trousers. Then, with the count on "Black Jack" Barry, demon of the pinch, one ball and one strike, Barry singled to left, scoring Gardner. Thomas singled to center and Barry moved to second, but Foster lifted a light fly to Luderus.

Speaker Gets Safe Blow

When Mayer was removed on the tail of Hooper's homer, Scott's line fly to Paskert, and Speaker's single in the third, and the appearance of the huge Rixey, Carrigan withdrew Hoblitzel while Dock was up at the plate. Hobby is a left-handed hitter, while Del Gainer hits from the other side of the plate. Gainer relieved Hoblitzel of his stick and hit to Bancroft, who stepped swiftly over to second, forcing out Speaker and then doubling up Gainer with a quick throw to first.

This tied the score, but after Cravath had fanned in the fourth, Luderus put his wallop over the wall. Bert Niehoff, the luckless Colorado boy, got his first hit of the series—a single to center—after Whitted had gone out. Eddie Burns singled to right and Niehoff moved to third ahead of Hooper's throw, which bounded away from Gardner to the box seats just behind third.

Niehoff might have scored on that throw, but Pat Moran held him at third. Gardner retrieved the ball and hurled it into Thomas at the plate while Niehoff was still scuffling around third, recovering his balance, and this throw of Gardner's was also wild. Then Niehoff went on in across the plate. Burns got to second, but Gardner made a stand play on Rixey's roller and got his man at third.

Bancroft Makes Error

With two out in the sixth Bancroft gave Barry two bases on a bad throw. Forrest Cady was then announced as hitting for Thomas, and about that time a policeman came out and handed Bill Klem a note. The note evidently pertained to ground rules, as the announcer megaphoned the proclamation that only two bases would be allowed on an overthrow. Cady walked, the crowd complaining at a couple of Klem's decisions, but Niehoff tossed out Foster.

In the eighth, with two out, Cravath walked and Dugey ran for him, Luderus was hit by a pitched ball as Dugey started to steal second, but Silk O'Loughlin was watching the runner and not the plate and he waved Dugey out at second, as the ball reached Barry from Cady. Klem called O'Loughlin's attention to the fact that Luderus had been hit, however, and Dugey returned to second, only to see Whitted hit by Foster for an easy out.

It was then that Alexander was seen warming up again, and why Moran did not install him at this juncture will probably ever remain a mystery, Bealx Becker, the one-time Giant, went to right field in Cravath's place, and the game passed on to the riotous conclusion.

After Hooper's homer, Bancroft made a good stop and a bad throw on Scott's grounder, and Luderus had to pull a curious catch to retire the runner. Speaker fanned but Burns dropped the ball, and had to throw out the Texan.

In the Philadelphia club's last stab at that extra $1,200 per man, and the world's championship title, Niehoff fanned. Burns grounded to Gainer, and was retired by the first baseman unassisted. Bill Killifer, the star catcher of the Phillies, out of the series because of a bad shoulder, made his first appearance, batting in place of Rixey, but Bill walloped the first ball pitched to him at Scott and was thrown out at first.

The ball clubs were delayed in getting from Boston for several hours by an accident to their train down in New Jersey. For a time there was a suggestion of rain in the banks of dark clouds that massed against the distant skyline, but the weather remained perfect, giving this series at least one record from start to finish.

Washington Herald
October 20, 1915

Coffey Beaten By Frank Moran

Blond Pittsburgh Battler Hangs Punch on Dublin Giant's jaw in Third

Kayoed On His Feet

With a swinging right-hand smash to the celebrated "glass" jaw, that followed fast on top of a left-hand jab to an already badly damaged eye, Frank Moran knocked Jim Coffey, the Irish giant, groveling on his face in the rosin dust of the ring at Madison Square Garden tonight.

About a minute and thirty-eight seconds of the third round had passed when the blond Pittsburgher connected. He had been craftily fiddling for some time to get that wallop across. He had taken poke after poke in the face from Coffey's left, but closing in and smothering Coffey's right, and always watchfully waiting with that one big punch.

He got it through in the second round and had Coffey drunk on the ropes, but the Irishman recovered. In the third, with 10,000 people all apparently yelling for Coffey, the Pittsburgh man again connected. Down went Coffey on his face. He staggered to his feet as Referee Brown counted three, and clung to the ropes. Moran rushed upon him and started a swing, but Brown pulled him away and pushed the dazed Coffey to his corner. The face of the Irishman was bruised and discolored. His eyes were heavy as with a great sleep. He was out, standing up.

Voluble, and angry, Billy Gibson, Coffey's manager, rushed about the ring, denouncing the action of the referee.

"Who ever heard of a man being declared out when he is on his feet?" he demanded. "Brown didn't give us a count."

Another punch would surely have knocked Coffey cold. There was no reason for Brown permitting it to be delivered.

That crushing smash to the jaw ended the fight to all intents and purposes. And Moran began working toward the end in the second round. He let Coffey fight himself out in that round, giving way with head and body to the Irishman's every punch while the packed galleries howled for the pride of Roscommon. Then, in the next round, the Pittsburgher began cutting down his man.

He knew too much for the big Irishman. Veteran of many a long hard battle, the Pennsylvanian had no difficulty in working Coffey around to just where he wanted him. Moran does not give any particular impression of grace or effectiveness, at first, but he soon developed the latter. When he cut loose with his right, Coffey rocked from head to foot.

Over in his corner, Gibson and old black Joe Jeannette were yelling advice at him, but Jim's eyes were glazing and his legs were limber. He covered weakly under the second round assault, and came up apparently fresh enough for the third round, but he was soon wobbling again, and Moran pressed relentlessly forward with left-hand jabs and right-hand clouts.

They clinched once in the second, with Moran grinning confidently over Coffey's shoulder. They tussled to the center of the ring, and after a little more fiddling, during which Moran even swung that right at a "ready." The Pittsburgh man shot out his left. The brittle jaw of Coffey went back, wide open—then whang! Down went the hope of Roscommon. The right hand of Moran had lifted and dropped forward like a hammer.

Gibson claims Coffey was not in distress. He says if his corner had thought so a towel would have gone in, but to the spectators it seemed that the Irishman was far enough "out" to justify the action of Brown.

Jim might have recovered—but not Tuesday night. He made a game fight and he lost. That's all there is to it.

Washington Herald
October 27, 1915

Johnny Dundee The Winner Of Battle

New York Lightweight Defeats Willies Ritchie, Former Title Holder, in Ten Rounds

Johnny Dundee beat Willie Ritchie, former lightweight champion of the world, in their bout at Madison Square Garden tonight, and beat him through all but two of the ten rounds.

The queer hop-toad tactics of the little Italian seemed to completely befuddle the one-time title-holder. Willie was more of a welterweight than a lightweight on the scales, having nearly ten pound's advantage over Dundee, and he was more of a second-rater than a champion in the ring. A fast and clever boxer at his best, there were moments tonight when he seemed painfully slow and loggy before the weird-squatting, hopping, bouncing attack of the Italian.

In the eighth the Californian appeared to finally be getting unlimbered, and he caught Dundee on the tip of the jaw with a right-hand lick that knocked Johnny to the ropes, following this a second later with another slashing right that staggered Dundee. In the ninth he unveiled a beautiful right cross, catching Dundee fair on the jaw, but the Italian proved that there is no glass in his facial structure by shaking off the punch and then winning the round.

Ritchie was cautioned for holding by Bill Brown in the fourth. In the fifth the fighters fell in a heap when Johnny almost hurdled Ritchie in a wild rush. Once Willie slipped and fell on the wet canvas, the rain falling through the open skylight and dampening the surroundings. Through the earlier stages of the fight Ritchie fought in a dazed manner and let Dundee swarm all over him. But in the concluding rounds he was fighting with something like the form that once made him champion.

He has no chance to catch up, however. Dundee tried to make every round a winning round, and won too far away for any argument.

Omaha Daily Bee
December 12, 1915

Gotham Gets Info on One J. Stecher

Jack Curley and Yousiff Hussane Return to New York and Spill News to Damon Runyon

And Damon Puts It in Paper

Yousouf Hussane, the Turk wrestler, and Jack Curley, his manager, have returned from Lincoln, Neb., where Hussane was beaten on Thanksgiving day by Joe Stecher, the new western mat marvel. Stecher won in two straight falls, devoting about four minutes to the subject of the sultan the first time and slightly more than that for the second fall.

When interrogated about the matter up in Curley's office, Hussane walked the floor, flailing the air above his head with his arms.

"Oh-o-o-o, I am so nervous," he said. "Oh-o-o-oyes, yes! Somedings it happens. I do not know. No? I am so nervous! Hussane, he is defeat in nine minuytes. What a business is this! It better was that i be drunk. I could not have done worser. Nine minyutes! Hussane! Oh-o-o-o! I am so nervous!"

"He hasn't quite recovered yet," said Curley. "Stecher got him with a scissors hold for the first fall--that hold with the two legs around the body which the Nebraskan has perfected to murderous efficiency. The second time Hussane got behind him, and was working on him, when suddenly one of Stecher's ham-like hands shot out, grasping Hussane around the wrist, and threw him around in the air. It was all oveer so quickly that i could scarcely realize what had happened. As for Hussane--well, you see him."

"I am so nervous," said Hussane, walking the floor.

"Hussane s a good wrestler, and had you told me any man in the world could throw him twice in nine minutes I'd have laughed at you," continued Curley. "This Stecher is the greatest wrestler I've ever seen. In my opinion, he is the greatest anybody has ever seen. If ever he meets Gotch, and he probably will within the next year, out around Omaha, I'm going to bet all I can borrow or beg on Stecher."

"I should shoost as well be drunk; I could not have done worser," insisted Hussane.

Joe Is a Farmer

"Stecher is 23 years old, and was born and reared in the little town of Dodge, Neb.," resumed Curley. "I never heard of Dodge before in my life until I heard of Stecher, but I am told that another of our American great wrestlers, Clarence Whistler, came from there. I always thought he originated in Baltimore, but it seems not.

"Stecher never had a wrestling lesson in his life. All he knows about the game he has picked up himself, and if he can beat Gotch, as I think he can, it will be one of the most wonderful accomplishments in the history of wrestling.

"Stecher is not an exceedingly big fellow, being of medium height and weighing about 190 pounds, but he is amazingly strong and fast on the mat. All his preliminary wrestling was done with his brother and sister out on the farm. They tell me his sister can easily throw the average wrestler.

"The scissors hold apparently came natural to Stecher, but he has perfected it in many ways. When he trains he takes a sack stuffed full of wheat and straddles it, bringing the pressure of his legs to bear upon it until the bag bursts. I've heard it said, too, that he used to straddle cows and horses, and crumple them up by the terrific pressure of his limbs; but this story sounds a bit far fetched.

"Stecher has never wrestled an exhibition. When he steps on the mat he is out to win, and he wins so quickly that it really isn't much of a show. He has thrown eight men in seventy-eight minutes in his last eight matches—sixteen falls. Why, any man in this wrestling tournament that is going on here now would be a mark for him, in my opinion."

"I am so nervous," remarked Hussane.

Curley Shows How

"Here!" said Curley, suddenly grabbing Bill Farnsworth, who wandered into the office at that luckless moment, "I'll show you how Stecher took Hussane on the second fall." And before the astounded Bill knew what was coming off he was down on the floor and the industrious Jack was using him as a lay figure to illustrate his lecture.

We have seen and heard "Hurry-Up" Yost reel off one of his movie scenarios of a football game, and we have observed George Stallings at full speed in a baseball conversazione, but they have nothing on Jack Curley when the topic is wrestling. Jack Herman, a Chicago wrestling promoter, who is now bringing the original Zbyszko back to this country, came in and added to Prof. Curley's audience.

"He's thrown such men as Cutler and Westergaard and Americus without the slightest trouble," said Curley, meaning Stecher. "When he wrestled Cutler a big chunk of money went out of Chicago to bet on Cutler. I know of over $20,000 from one source that was gathered in by the Nebraska farmers. At that time the wise lads in the wrestling game thought he was a sucker, but they've changed their minds. Gotch had a bet on Cutler."

"He's pretty good, that Stecher," affirmed Herman. "I've seen him work. Still, it seems to me that most of the fellows he has wrestled were made to order for that scissors—rather thin fellows, mostly. I don't see how he could get his legs around Zbyszko, he's such an abnormally big man."

Can Beat 'Em All

"Mark what I tell you," said Curley. "Stecher will beat him sure. And you can take half a million dollars out there and they'll cover it for you. After Stecher had beaten a couple of chaps, a telegram came from Minneapolis, the home of Henry Ordeman, to a man in Nebraska asking if there was a chance to get a match for Ordeman under an assumed name.

"'We don't care anything about the gate, as we'll win enough on the side,' said the telegram.

"They thought up in Minneapolis that Ordeman's reputation would frighten Stecher people, but the fellow who got it showed it to Stecher, and he said:

"'Send them an answer telling them to bring Ordeman along under his right name and we'll wrestle him.' They never heard any more of the matter.

"We had an argument before the Lincoln match," Jack went on. "Hussane always wrestles with his feet bare and they wanted him to put on shoes. The debate continued until we got in the ring, and then Stecher ended it by telling Hussane to wrestle as he pleased. I wish they'd insist on the shoes. Then I'd have an alibi. Don't make any mistake on this fellow. I've been in the wrestling game many a year and he's the greatest I ever saw—bar none."

"I am so nervous," declared Hussane.

from

The Archive

Theodore Roosevelt: Wilderness, Vol. 1
ISBN: 978-0-9907137-1-5
List Price: $24.95
In the western states and territories a young Theodore Roosevelt found inspiring loneliness and a hunters' paradise. As "open season" on buffalo, antelope, mountain goat and white-tailed deer brought these species close to extinction, however, he began to understand the meaning and value of conservation—a progression expressed eloquently in the articles he penned for Century, The Outlook and other journals.

Richard Harding Davis: Journalism
ISBN: 978-0-9907137-4-6
List Price: $24.95
The year was 1897, and the place was the front page of Hearst's New York Journal. With "The Death of Adolfo Rodriguez," Richard Harding Davis created a sensation -- and public outrage that helped bring about the Spanish-American War. This collection of 25 original newspaper and magazine stories, complete and unabridged, offers the reader a front page seat to compelling events all over the globe, and newspaper reporting as done with literary skill, social conscience and a flair for the dramatic.

Nellie Bly: Undercover: Reporting for *The New York World* **1887-1894**
ISBN: 978-0-9907137-2-2
List Price: $24.95

Nellie Bly's convincing disguises gained her admission to oppressive sweatshops, underground gambling parlors, illicit adoption agencies and creepy mesmerists' parlors, all in the service of sensational headlines and the steadily rising circulation numbers boasted by the New York World. This fascinating collection of original, unabridged articles—compiled for the first time since their original publication--traces Bly's brief yet astounding career as an undercover journalist.

Reporting: The Tulsa Riot
ISBN: 978-0-9907137-5-3
List Price: $27.95

On June 1, 1921, an awkward encounter in a small elevator spiraled into the deadliest riot in American history. After two days of burning, looting, killing and mayhem in Tulsa, the reported death toll stood at "unknown (possibly hundreds)" and an entire neighborhood--Tulsa's prospering African-American enclave of Greenwood--had been looted, bombed, and reduced to smoldering ruins.

    Published by The Archive of American Journalism, this collection of contemporary newspaper and magazine articles brings readers a street-level view of the events in Tulsa. Through dozens of newspaper bulletins, firsthand accounts, in-depth investigations, interviews, telegraph dispatches, editorials and opinion pieces, this first volume in The Archive's unique Reporting series holds up a mirror to the city, its social and economic conflicts, and the wider rifts in American society.

from
www.historicjournalism.com

"For years and years California's position on the Chinese question has been conspicuously contemptible. We have been imploring Congress to save us from ourselves—to avert from our undeserving heads the consequences of our own selfishness. We have prayed that the Chinese might be kept away from us, in order that we might not hurt ourselves by employing them. Within the past fifteen years I have myself repeatedly submitted, with all due deference, that we need not employ them nor purchase of them if we did not wish, and that we merited no outside assistance so long as we did. Others spoke to the same effect, but we were a feeble and unheeded few.

"All eyes were turned to Washington, all hopes were centered in Congress. It is not surprising that the relief we got was grudgingly given, for our sincerity was open to disproof. If there had been no Congress to help us we should long ago have helped ourselves. But for our own apathy and greed there would not be today enough Chinamen in California to carry a lightweight Polish refugee into the Board of Education."

Ambrose Bierce
"Prattle," *The Wasp*, April 3, 1886

"While waiting for the game to begin the National Commission got together and decided the place of the seventh game, if it is necessary to play a seventh. Garry Herrmann, chairman of the commission, tossed a coin, and Harry Hempstead, president of the

Giants, gave Charley Comiskey the call. The "Old Roman" called heads and the coin fell tails.

"It was the first time Hempstead had won a toss. He missed three straight calls in tossing for the opening game.

"On that occasion the coin twice fell off a table. This time Hempstead insisted on having it tossed on the floor. 'I don't want any more tables,' he said."

Damon Runyon, "White Sox Rally, Defeating Giants in Erratic Game," *Washington Herald*, October 14, 191

"New York Noveletic: Broadway is flooded with ambitious youth. Such were this stage-struck girl and newcomer-wrighter—ambitious in love . . . You can see hundreds of them in New York making park benches their thrones, holding hands in movie balconies or chop-suey joints—walking along the Drive, drinking in the moon and stars—not saying a word—while music runs through their veins and their hearts dance . . . All they hope, pray and hunger for is success. They want life to hug them and make their cheeks bloom . . . Two young people in a strange town finding a home in each other's memory. Well, one day she got a bit part in a show, clicked and was whisked off to Hollywood . . . He went into an ad agency.

"For a while love letters were swapped at a fast clip, then the traffic slowed down, limped along, and finally ceased . . . Love had "taken a powder" . . . A run-out . . . They were riding to the moon on their careers, they couldn't think of anything else . . . Soon, Christmas cards were their only contact. And now they both have everything they came to New York to get—dreams come true . . . But they are not as happy as they were when they had nothing—except each other."

Walter Winchell, "New York Heartbeat," *New York Daily Mirror,* May 3, 1940

"Apparently those in each boat were selected by lot . . .The only other persons originally in my boat were Red Cross nurses of the Post unit and infants. In trampling upon them to safety I foresaw no difficulty. But at the dress rehearsal the purser added six dark and dangerous-looking Spaniards. It developed later that by profession they were bull-fighters. Any man who is not afraid of a bull is entitled to respect. But being cast adrift with six did not appeal. One could not help wondering what would happen if we ran out of provisions and the bull-fighters grew hungry. I tore up my ticket and planned to swim."

Richard Harding Davis, "President Poincare Thanks America," *The New York Times*, November 6, 1916

7

www.ingramcontent.com/pod-product-compliance
Lightning Source LLC
Chambersburg PA
CBHW020429010526
44118CB00010B/500